LIBERAL ARTS POWER!

LIBERAL ARTS POWER!

What It Is and How to Sell It on Your Resume

Second Edition

Burton Jay Nadler

Peterson's Guides
Princeton, New Jersey

Library of Congress Cataloging-in-Publication Data

Nadler, Burton Jay, 1953–
    Liberal arts power! : what it is and how to sell it on your resume / Burton Jay Nadler. — 2nd ed.
      p.   cm.
    Includes bibliographical references.
    ISBN 0-87866-880-2
    1. Résumés (Employment).
2. Education, Humanistic. I. Title.
HF5383.N3 1989
650.14—dc20   89-23099
                           CIP

Composition and design by Peterson's Guides

Printed in the United States of America

10 9 8 7 6 5 4 3 2 1

In 1985 I dedicated the first edition of this book to a number of very special people:

To all of the students who asked, "Do you have a few minutes to look at my resume?"
Each minute spent critiquing your resumes contributed to an ever-increasing understanding of the resume-writing and job search processes. With this book I am now able to share with others what you have taught me.

To Terry.
You took a chance and hired someone whose resume reflected limited experience and you showed me that career planning and placement is a career field with numerous rewards.

To Teri.
We have shared several job searches, each of which resulted in success and in continued professional development. You are proof that a liberal arts job seeker can be successful at whatever she does.

To Jordan.
Your resume is very, very brief right now. I can't wait to see the entries that the future will bring.

I also want to offer a special word of thanks to the following individuals: Grant Bogle, Russ Dunham, Kevin Kruse, Tim Plunkett, Robert Smith, K. Vinton Taylor, and Lisa Bowers White. These recruiting professionals reviewed many of the sample resumes that appear in this book, offering some very constructive feedback, and provided their own basic views about hiring liberal arts graduates. In addition, my thanks go to these recruiters for hiring many of the liberal arts job seekers I have worked with over the years.

Upon the publication of the second edition of this work, I would like to add the following.

To those who have taught me valuable lessons related to applying my liberal arts skill and talents to human resources management on "the corporate side."
Because of what you have taught me I am more knowledgeable about my own capabilities and about the opportunities and challenges you offer others. As a result, I am a better human resources professional and a better career counselor and job search coach.

To Justin.
Like your sister's, your resume started out very brief. Both of you are experiencing many, many new things each day of your lives. Jordan and Justin, the excitement I feel about sharing those experiences that will be future entries grows as you do.

Contents

Preface

Almost everyone associates resume writing and resumes with a job search and in some way realizes that the process and its end product are critical to success. The never-ending requests for reactions to resume drafts that I encountered during my tenure in career services were evidence that even the most uninitiated job seekers knew that writing a resume was important. I was always ready to offer my advice, and, perhaps more important, to turn first requests for assistance into solid foundations upon which meaningful career counseling relationships could be built. For me, and for many of those I worked with over the years, resume writing is not simply an independent act but part of a larger series of interdependent actions that, taken together, result in job search success.

From the first person I saw as a full-time career services professional through the countless number of students, alumni, friends, and others I counseled, my belief in resume writing as the right way to initiate a job search effort *and* to learn job hunting skills has strengthened. As I worked with more and more people—individuals with varied academic and personal backgrounds—I identified and fine-tuned some key elements of my counseling style and philosophy. By sharing the following personal "trade secrets," I hope to offer some insight into the philosophy underlying this book:

- Resume writing should be linked to other job search activities, including self-assessment, goal setting, employer contact, networking, and interviewing. The total process, like creating a resume, can be divided into realistic and clearly defined action steps. Actions, not printed documents, are the most essential components of job search success.

- Job seekers should regard resumes as constantly evolving; they should feel free to make changes or develop more than one version. While resumes are subject to constant constructive criticism, the decision whether to change a resume rests solely with the job seeker.

- Once motivated to get started (by an individual, a publication, or an event), the sooner a job seeker develops a first draft and has it reviewed, the better. Resume writing can be a reason to begin, not to put off, the process of job search.

- Sample resumes can be instrumental in motivating job seekers to write first drafts and fine-tune subsequent ones, but they should not be projected as "the right way" to create resumes. While rules of thumb and standards of acceptable quality exist, samples should inspire, not limit, resume writers.

- Resumes should be viewed as multipurpose documents, essential for, but not limited to, job search activities. Resumes can be used in various situations, such as applying to graduate school or applying for membership in a professional organization, and a current one should always be available.

• Although each job seeker has unique qualities, is subject to different pressures, and confronts varying job search circumstances, counselors still need to pay attention to the needs of special groups, among them liberal arts majors. These needs and the wide range of fields of employment available to liberal arts majors cannot be ignored when developing a resume or when beginning any job search effort.

While I have worked with job seekers (college seniors, recent and not-so-recent alumni, and others) of almost every academic background—undergraduate and graduate business, communications, computer science, education, engineering, journalism, and fine arts majors—I have always felt a special professional responsibility for and, yes, kinship with those with liberal arts backgrounds. I am sure this is in part because of my own academic history and because of the large proportion of liberal arts students on campuses where I have worked. It is also because liberal arts majors are frequently subject to the frustrating consequences of stereotyping and negative press. The portrayal of liberal arts majors as job search underdogs has instilled in me a desire to champion this cause and to project realities rather than stereotypes.

Also, as a result of the efforts of academic institutions to address decreasing enrollment in liberal arts departments and to emphasize the virtues of a liberal education, my colleagues and I have in recent years been able to create career programs and approaches for this particular group. Many have become sensitive to the needs of liberal arts majors and have, in a variety of ways, worked toward strengthening interest in the humanities, arts, and social sciences, striving to preserve a more humanistic and less pragmatic view of education. I am pleased to have been associated with a number of these organizations and individuals as a counselor, author, speaker, and recruiter.

In the effort to define "a liberal arts major," some cite *inclusive* fields or departments: "English and literature as well as the social, physical, and natural sciences." Others look at *exclusive* areas: "business, computer science, and engineering," and identify liberal arts as all remaining curricula. You will never find universal agreement. I take an *operational* approach: a liberal arts major for me, as well as for the purposes of this book, is an individual who can, *if desired* (and most likely only after a great deal of graduate study), add the suffixes *"ian"* or *"ist"* or the word *"teacher"* after his or her major field to determine the most stereotypical career option. While this is an interesting exercise, many have been and continue to be frustrated because they do *not* want to be histor**ian**s, psycholog**ist**s, or English **teacher**s. A liberal arts major, then, must determine his or her own career alternatives and take greater responsibility for setting goals and developing strategies. Therefore, the needs of liberal arts job seekers go beyond the development and application of standardized job search tools and techniques to the creation of new attitudes and the utilization of specialized approaches. My counseling experiences taught me a great deal, and it has always been a personal and professional goal to share this knowledge with others—to extend my counsel beyond the limitations of an appointment book. Thanks to organizations like Peterson's, one of the strongest supporters of the liberal arts, this publication and my other works exist today.

This book began life as a proposal entitled "I Majored in Psychology, But Did Not Want to Be a Psychologist," reflecting my suffix-oriented definition of career goal setting and job search, as well as my personal interest in a particular group of students and alumni. After my discussions with editors at Peterson's the proposal was redefined (and I must admit improved), resulting in a very large manuscript encompassing resume writing, job options, and job search techniques for all liberal arts majors. The resume-writing and cover letter portions were culled and edited into *Liberal Arts Power!* (Peterson's Guides, 1985), with goal setting, job options, and job search approaches appearing in *Liberal Arts Jobs* (Peterson's Guides, 1986). While these two works found their origins in one manuscript and were intended to be used together, they seemed to be most often utilized independently. Both were well received by job seekers and career services professionals, meeting the needs of liberal arts majors and those who counsel them.

While more institutions, professionals, and authors have, since 1985, directed their resources and energies toward assisting liberal arts majors, with greater attention have come higher expectations. The need of liberal arts majors for additional and improved information and support services has increased. As a response to this heightened demand, and because of our (mine and Peterson's) wish to share the knowledge gained over the past four-plus years, the decision was made to revise *Liberal Arts Power!* and *Liberal Arts Jobs*.

With the revisions of 1989 both works are again linked and, I trust, in many ways improved. Throughout each work you will see references to the other, with many concepts and a few exercises appearing in both. While the new editions can be used independently, much can be gained by using both. Ideally, one would read *Liberal Arts Jobs* first, set goals and become familiar with job search techniques, then read *Liberal Arts Power!* to develop the resume and become versed in writing effective job search correspondence. At this point, one could go back and forth using portions of each text as needed throughout the job search. We all know the world is far from ideal, so if you are currently interested only in resume writing and job search correspondence, this work will suffice. But do not hesitate to refer to *Liberal Arts Jobs* when you wish additional information.

Now that we have discussed the linkage of both publications, let's focus on what this book is designed to do. *Liberal Arts Power!* will:

- Increase your understanding of where your resume and job search correspondence fit in the job search process.

- Provide you with enough information and direction, through text, exercises, sample resumes, and more, to enable you to develop dynamic and effective resumes and job search correspondence.

- Share the resume development and job search stories of numerous liberal arts majors, reinforcing the realistic and positive attitudes required for success.

You already have liberal arts power; now put it to work for you.

Burt Nadler
September 1989

What Is Liberal Arts Power?

It's about time that the myths associated with liberal arts graduates and the job hunt get cleared up once and for all!

Students, parents, career counselors, and placement professionals continue to hear about the so-called "plight of the liberal arts graduate." Each year (most likely around graduation time), newspaper and magazine articles and television and radio reports make much of the "fact" that liberal arts students are becoming less and less marketable, that they are having greater difficulty securing employment after graduation. Well, it's about time that the myths associated with liberal arts graduates and the job hunt get cleared up once and for all!

My experience has shown me that liberal arts job seekers may have difficulty getting started but that, once they are armed with the right job search tools, an understanding of how to implement an effective job search campaign, and the positive attitudes required for success in any endeavor, they have no trouble finding and keeping excellent jobs. Liberal arts graduates have the qualifications employers seek, and, whether they know it or not, they all have the capacity to market these qualifications successfully.

Unfortunately, however, many talented people begin their job search filled with self-doubt and anxiety. Having heard too many horror stories about the "unemployable" liberal arts graduate, they too often come to believe that they have no marketable skills to offer an employer and that their credentials are not strong enough for them to be able to carry out a winning job search. The simple truth is that far too many liberal arts graduates are victims of a self-fulfilling prophecy. Fearing the future and not really expecting to be successful, they make timid and ineffective efforts at finding a job. Because they make such a poor start, they often do encounter difficulty, and too many end up either unemployed or, what may be worse, underemployed, having settled for jobs beneath their capabilities.

Liberal arts graduates have proven that they can find jobs that are just as challenging and rewarding as the work secured by their peers who majored in other disciplines. It is true that if one looks at broad statistics, such as the number of recruiting organizations that request interviews with liberal arts graduates or the average salary offers for liberal arts graduates, it is easy to be pessimistic. But if one focuses on each liberal arts job seeker as a person who is capable of finding satisfying employment, a truer picture begins to emerge.

Unlike students in preprofessional or vocational programs, liberal arts majors generally need to go through a process of self-assessment before they can become really effective job seekers, and they must research careers in order to identify goals. As noted in the Preface, those who do not wish to become *"ians," "ists,"* or *teachers* must transcend these stereotypical limitations and take action to define research, job search, and, when appropriate, career goals. *Liberal Arts Jobs,* the companion volume to this book, begins with the process of goal formation, elaborates upon the differences among these three types of goals, and provides information on over 300 career options. When focused and armed with an effective resume and the positive attitude required for success, liberal arts graduates have no trouble finding excellent jobs.

In order to succeed in the job search, however, liberal arts students must learn to be self-directed and to implement aggressive job-hunting techniques. They have to adopt a new mind-set. They should not, for example, expect to be recruited directly off the college campus for their first job. Although many students do find employment through the on-campus recruiting system, expecting that this will automatically be the case will only serve to perpetuate the previously discussed self-fulfilling prophecy.

It is the job seeker who must present himself or herself as being qualified for a particular position; the degree and the major are relatively unimportant.

Liberal arts job seekers must learn to go directly to employers rather than wait for employers to come to them. These students should certainly participate as much as possible in on-campus recruiting programs, since many large corporations, retailers, banks, consulting firms, and manufacturers do recruit liberal arts graduates, but they should not depend solely on this process to find a job.

It is important to remember that it is the job seeker who must present himself or herself as being qualified for a particular position; the degree and the major are relatively unimportant. Career counselors commonly hear comments like these from liberal arts majors: "I haven't done anything!" . . . "What can I put on a resume?" . . . "What can I tell an interviewer?" In most cases, these people are far too critical about their own past, judging important events as "not worth noting on a resume." It is as if they wish to categorize accomplishments as irrelevant before a potential employer has the chance to do so. These individuals have accepted what they have heard and read about liberal arts graduates having little to offer an employer, and, by being overcritical, they are compounding their anxiety and self-doubt.

In order to write an effective resume and carry out a successful job search, liberal arts job seekers must, at best, be confident and self-assured and, at the very least, objective about their abilities and accomplishments. Employers will judge experiences according to their own criteria. Your job is to show how your skills and experiences have prepared you for the job. Your job is to *sell* your liberal arts power.

While it may be difficult to define what constitutes a liberal arts major, most of us can readily identify the qualities and capabilities associated with liberal arts students and graduates. The following are usually on any list of traits possessed by liberal arts majors.

- Written communication skills
- Interpersonal skills
- Oral communication skills
- Adaptability
- Well-developed work habits
- Decision-making skills
- Research skills
- Analytical orientation
- Interdisciplinary perspective
- Exposure to diverse points of view
- Exposure to different cultural environments and languages

Few will argue that these are not valuable characteristics, but it is important to emphasize just how desirable they are to employers and for liberal arts majors to understand how they can use them to become effective job seekers. When an annual and much-respected study (Michigan State's "Recruiting Trends 1988–89") called upon recruiters to identify qualifications that would make new college graduates more productive and ready for employment, a rank ordering of fifty-three traits was established. The first six in the above list appeared in the top ten of this survey, and many of the fifty-three traits identified are associated with liberal arts graduates. (I refer you to this study for additional information and, perhaps more important, for motivation.)

Liberal arts power is a blending of ability, attitude, and, most important, action.

Liberal arts power is the possession of many of these qualities and, as a result, the ability to research options, set goals, and project ideas and qualifications on paper and in person. It is the utilization of skills that have, by virtue of broad and more "liberal" academic experiences, been ingrained and honed in every liberal arts major. These allow the liberal arts major to accomplish job search–related tasks, including resume writing, and to convince a potential employer that the skills one possesses are related to on-the-job performance.

Liberal arts power can also be defined as a positive yet realistic belief in oneself. It is acceptance of the fact that liberal arts majors seeking employment are more responsible for communicating goals and projecting qualifications than are those graduating with vocationally oriented majors. The field of study that a liberal arts major has pursued does not project the employment-related skills a liberal arts job seeker has to offer, nor does it project job search or career goals. Therefore, it is the responsibility of liberal arts majors to identify these goals and present to others the qualifications they possess to perform job-related tasks. While awareness of this responsibility is important, it is even more important that liberal arts job seekers be aware that they possess the "response-ability" to succeed. By properly utilizing the skills and capabilities noted above, liberal arts majors can meet the challenges of the job search and employment and will continue to prove the value of a liberal arts education throughout their careers. Liberal arts power, then, is a blending of ability, attitude, and, most important, action.

After you have done your homework and made the connections between your abilities and the requirements of a particular job, you will feel confident and "liberal arts powerful." Self-criticism and self-doubt recede when you know you have something to offer, when you see your own liberal arts power on your resume.

The resume plays a very important part in the liberal arts graduate's job search. A good resume will bear a bit of the burden of job hunting for you and it should increase your confidence as well. It will present your liberal arts power on paper and prepare you to present your liberal arts power in person.

The secret to carrying out a successful job search thus lies in the art of marketing oneself and one's skills confidently and with imagination. Liberal arts graduates must develop individualized job search strategies; they must believe in their abilities to perform tasks associated with the jobs they want; and they must project confidence to all of the employers they communicate with. One of the principal ways of doing all of this—that is, of marketing oneself effectively—is by developing the best resume possible.

This book will help you overcome the psychological barriers that may be stopping you from writing a resume and pursuing a successful job search.

My work as a career counselor at several colleges and universities and in private practice has convinced me that once liberal arts job seekers have taken the time to assess their skills and to tailor their resumes to reflect their capabilities and direction, they begin to realize just how powerful they can be. They come to understand that they have their own brand of marketing power—their "liberal arts power"—and that it can be used just as effectively as the credentials presented by graduates of preprofessional or vocational programs.

This book is meant to educate and to motivate. It will show you how to make the connections between your abilities and the requirements of a particular job and how to present them on your resume. The sample resumes and accompanying analyses will show you what is required to develop an effective resume of your own. The information and advice offered throughout the book will help you overcome the psychological barriers that may be stopping you from writing a resume and pursuing a successful job search. This book can be used by first-time job seekers as well as by those who are seeking career changes and new jobs.

It is my hope that this book and the job search success stories of its readers will begin to counteract the myth of the unemployability of the liberal arts graduate. Self-perpetuating negativism has hurt too many people and hindered too many job searches. It is now time to create realistic and positive attitudes and to write about success stories rather than horror stories. By starting to read this book, you have begun to write your own success story.

The Job Search and the Resume

By coming to terms with the job search process and devising a creative and well-written resume, all liberal arts graduates can realize the goals of a liberal education.

Let's return to the original meaning of *artes liberales*—"work befitting a free man." This book is intended to help liberal arts graduates find satisfying work. Because they are truly free to enter any one of numerous career fields, liberal arts graduates must make careful decisions about career goals and adopt special job-hunting strategies. By coming to terms with the job search process and devising a creative and well-written resume, all liberal arts graduates can realize the goals of a liberal education—ongoing self-expression and self-fulfillment. This book, by design, discusses resume writing within the broader context of the job search. While much can be learned about skills assessment, goal setting, job search correspondence, and interviewing from the exercises and discussions that follow, I again refer to *Liberal Arts Jobs* as a resource that can increase your overall knowledge of the job search. Specifically, I recommend you review the ten-step overview of the liberal arts job search. This yields insight into how you can translate knowledge of the employment process into a step-by-step approach to the job search.

As noted earlier, the liberal arts job seeker does in fact bear a greater burden of communicating career goals and qualifications than the graduate of a vocationally oriented curriculum. In most cases, a degree title, whether it is a bachelor's, master's, or doctoral degree, does not communicate to the potential employer what the liberal arts graduate truly has to offer and neither does his or her major.

Too many liberal arts students ask the question: "What can I do with a major in 'X'?" These students are, unfortunately, laboring under the common misconception that a person's major somehow determines the types of jobs for which he or she is qualified. This is simply not true. A major does not equate with a job or a set of jobs, and no one major, whether liberal arts, technical, or business, guarantees that a person will obtain a job. Employers judge candidates according to the skills they possess and their potential to perform functions associated with particular job titles and descriptions. Some employers state desired degrees and majors when posting jobs or when recruiting on college campuses, but liberal arts graduates who understand the job search process know that what is most important is having the required skills and taking the steps necessary to present themselves as qualified candidates. They have taken the responsibility for learning about themselves and the nature of the job search, and they understand that they have the response-ability to act effectively.

Whether you are a soon-to-be or a recent college graduate looking for your first job, a person seeking new challenges and rewards in a second or third job, someone wishing to change careers or reenter the work force after spending time at home, or a person who has been forced by circumstances beyond your control to look for a new job, you must understand the job search process. If you are aware of what employers are looking for, you will understand what you must do to be successful and why the burden of proving that you are qualified for employment rests on you and not on the title of your major—and you will begin to see the important role your resume can play.

The Employer's Search

To fill a particular job, a company establishes a set of qualifications it feels are desirable. Once these skills, areas of knowledge, characteristics, interests, and values are established, the company's recruiter searches for candidates who fit the bill. In some cases, these qualifications are specified in job descriptions, sign-up schedules for on-campus interviews, and want ads. In all cases, the person doing the hiring keeps them clearly in mind.

The burden of proving that you are qualified for employment rests on you, not on the title of your major.

The hirer reviews resumes and cover letters and interviews candidates for the available position. During interviews, the employer listens for statements about a job seeker's past experiences that reveal whether he or she has the skills and other qualifications being sought. Job seekers who seem qualified are granted consideration, and eventually one candidate is offered the job.

While this seems quite simple, and, in fact, it is, that does not mean that job hunting is easy. Looking for a job requires a great deal of work—it is one of the most physically and psychologically demanding efforts you will undertake. And although writing a good resume is one of the most important steps in the process, it is not the only step. You must be prepared to *use* your resume effectively and ride the emotional roller coaster of the job search—in some cases for several months—until you find the job that is right for you. Your search will be successful if you keep in mind not only what a potential employer is looking for but also how you, the liberal arts job seeker, can best represent yourself to those potential employers—through your resume.

There is NO Excuse for Not Writing Your Resume Now!

Why does writing a resume make people so apprehensive?

For too many people, writing a resume is a difficult, anxiety-provoking process that delays rather than advances their job search. Why does the idea of writing a resume make people so apprehensive? I have frequently heard such answers as these:

"Because I don't have anything to put on a resume. I haven't done very much. I'm not the president of any organization, and I haven't received any academic honors or awards. My work experience is not extensive. Nothing I put on a resume will impress an employer, so why write one?"

"Because it is hard for me to write about myself. I can't lie about what I have done, and I have never been very good at bragging, making something very ordinary appear special. If that's what I have to do to write a resume, I would rather not write one."

"Because writing a resume means that I will have to start looking for a job, and I am afraid of the pressures of a job search. I'd rather wait until I'm better prepared to face the task ahead."

"Because writing a resume is like studying for and taking a final exam. You really don't know what a professor is going to ask on the exam, and you don't know what an employer really wants to see on the resume. You put in so much time and effort; it's unnerving to work so hard and not know what the results will be."

"Because I don't know how to write a resume. I have heard so many different things about resumes that I am confused. My dad tells me one thing and the counselor at the placement office tells me another. Books on resume writing present such contradictory information that I don't know what to do. I'm afraid if I don't do it the right way, I'll be wasting my time and jeopardizing my chances of finding a good job."

My response to these statements is as follows:

Everyone has something to put on a resume. You may be judging your past experiences too harshly, or you may not have thoroughly reviewed your accomplishments and achievements. Once you have assessed your skills and researched career options, you will be prepared to develop a resume that presents you as a person qualified for the job you seek. And remember, employers will be impressed not only by what you have done but also by the way you communicate your goals and abilities.

Employers are impressed not only by what you have done but also by the way you communicate your goals and abilities.

You don't have to brag or lie on a resume, but you should describe your experiences and abilities as positively as possible. Resumes are positive documents, and employers want to see what you have done. You can objectively state the facts to an employer without any sleight of hand.

Resume writing should be a stimulating activity—one of the first steps on a journey that will end in your finding a challenging and rewarding job. The journey may not be easy, and it may take longer than you would like, but it will end in success. The longer you wait to begin, the more anxious you will get, and the longer it will take before you have that wonderful experience of saying yes to a job offer.

Resume writing is an art, not an exact science. You should feel confident that you can develop a resume that fits your own background and goals.

You may not know now what an employer wants to see on a resume, but, after a thorough self-assessment and exploration of careers, you will know what you want to say on your resume. Knowing the skills you possess and the functions involved in various jobs will enable you to define your employment goals and thus direct the content of your resume toward a particular field or job.

There is no one right way to write a resume. Resume writing is an art, not an exact science. You should therefore feel confident that you can develop a resume that is right for you, one that accurately presents your background and goals.

Using Your Resume

Like the clothes worn to an employment interview, your resume must project a positive image, and it must fit both you and the circumstances. If you are not comfortable with your resume—if you don't feel that it is the very best resume—then you will not be an effective job seeker. This book enables you to try on various resume styles, and it provides the information you need to create the best resume you can. You will, of course, continue to grow intellectually, emotionally, and experientially, and a resume that fits today may not next year, next month, or even next week, so you should always be prepared to change your resume as needed. After reading this book, you will have enough confidence in the resume you create to be an effective job seeker; you will also have enough confidence in your resume-writing skills to be able to change your resume when necessary.

Your resume will not get you a job; rather, it is a tool for you to use to get an interview and for you to use *during* the interview and follow-up stages of the job search. Remember, your resume and job search correspondence are reflections of your written communication skills (key liberal arts skills). They must project liberal arts power—ability and attitude expressed in actions. As you develop your resume, as you determine what actions are appropriate, you should keep in mind the functions it can serve. They are described on the following page.

Special Tips

The following sections of this book show how to write a resume that can be used for all of the job-hunting activities outlined on page 9. Because this work can be used by first-time job seekers as well as by those who are seeking career changes and new jobs, here are some brief tips for special groups of resume writers.

You Can Use Your Resume

• To initiate contact with a potential employer:
Accompanied by a cover letter, the resume will serve in many cases as the initial contact with a prospective employer. Because it is the first indication an employer will have of the type of work you are capable of doing, your resume must create a positive first impression.

• To provide a potential employer with a concise summary of education, experience, skills, and goals:
The resume is a device for imparting information—information concerning education, employment, extracurricular activities, and any other experiences that have contributed to the development of skills that qualify you for positions you want. You should do this as succinctly as possible but without omitting information that projects qualifications to an employer. Your resume should be the best representation of *all* that you have to offer. It should not be limited to an arbitrary page length, but it should be as brief as possible.

• To facilitate the employment interview by serving as a guide for both interviewer and interviewee:
The resume provides a common base of knowledge shared by you and the interviewer and can be used as a map to guide both of you through the two-way street that is the employment interview. The interviewer will ask you to elaborate upon information presented on the resume. You, in turn, can refer to it in order to cite examples of specific skills that are of interest to the employer. The better the resume, the more you can use it to ensure a successful interview.

• To share information with persons assisting in the job search:
The resume is an excellent way to inform others of your job search and solicit their help. You can use the resume to develop and maintain a contact network—a group of resource persons and references. Give copies of your resume to your contacts and ask them to distribute them as they learn about employment opportunities. Career counselors and others who provide assistance and information can use the resume to stay informed of your goals and qualifications. People who write letters of recommendation for you can refer to the resume in order to remind themselves of your specific qualities and accomplishments.

• To serve as a record to leave with a potential employer or resource person, so follow-up can be done effectively:
The resume is your calling card. You can leave it with prospective employers and resource persons to facilitate future communications. You can follow up with phone calls, letters, or visits and be confident that the recipient of the resume knows something about your background and goals. Most job offers are made during follow-up contacts.

• To supplement information when completing applications:
Most application forms request a great deal of information yet provide very little space in which to write. Whether you are applying for employment, admission to graduate or professional school, or membership in a professional organization, you can make sure that you are providing all the information required for a thorough consideration of your candidacy by attaching your resume to the application.

Freshmen and Sophomores Just Getting Started . . .

Most likely, you are developing a resume for a part-time-job or summer-job search. I urge you not to be concerned with what you *haven't* done but to focus on how best to highlight what you *have* accomplished. While you may not have a lengthy list of sophisticated work experiences, you should have a great many academic strengths. Don't be turned off by the accomplishment-filled samples that appear on subsequent pages. They illustrate the ways your resume *can,* not should, appear, with citations that time and effective job search will bring. Be aware that your face-to-face (in person), voice-to-ear (phone), and eye-to-paper (correspondence) interactions are crucial. Create a good resume now, but spend a great deal of time supporting it with actions and words. Liberal arts power is always best channeled if you have a focus. Identify one or two fields of interest and communicate to potential employers within these fields how much you wish to learn and what you are willing to give in return. Networking through family members, friends, and others (recruiters and alumni identified through the career planning and placement office of your school) should be done early and thoroughly.

Juniors Beginning to Think About Postgraduation Options . . .

You could be thinking that this is the last chance to obtain a great "resume-building" summer or part-time job. You're probably not thinking that this is a good time to begin some of the actions required of a successful job search next year, but you should be. For those concerned about their next part-time or summer job, the concept of resume building is best thought of as "skills building." Where you work (the name of the firm and the type of organization it is) can be important, but what you will be doing (the nature of daily activities) is more important. If you have not begun the self-assessment and research required to identify potential postgraduation options, *do so.* This will have a positive influence on your part-time-job and summer-job search as well as your future full-time-job efforts. I, again, refer you to *Liberal Arts Jobs* for the reasons noted earlier.

While most college students have financial pressures that require paying positions, especially in the summer between the junior and senior years, do not rule out the possibility of obtaining a nonpaying, career-related opportunity. This can be in addition to a paying position. Again, do not be too concerned with what you cannot put on your resume. Create the best resume possible and highlight academic, extracurricular, and employment strengths—but be aware that how you present yourself and how you support your resume are the keys to job search success. Use the spring and summer to conduct as many informational interviews as possible. The clearer your focus now and, most important, during the next year, the more liberal arts powerful you will be. Take advantage of the services offered by your school's career planning and placement office for your part-time-job or summer-job search, and learn about the services it will offer during your senior year. Learn from your friends who are seniors. They might provide good leads for your most immediate job search and, of course, they can offer insights into what lies ahead.

Seniors Getting Ready for the Job Search . . .

This book was written primarily with you in mind. You should get a great deal from it and from its companion publication, *Liberal Arts Jobs,* but don't forget about the resources that are available through your career planning and placement office. Don't fall into the trap of believing that these offices are only for business and engineering majors. While this impression can be based on a realistic appraisal of an on-campus recruiting schedule, it is not totally accurate. Learn about what these facilities offer and take advantage of their resources. Be liberal arts powerful with the proper assessment and projection of abilities by maintaining a positive attitude and by taking effective actions!

Recent Graduates Still Looking . . .

While you may feel isolated (if you have moved far from your alma mater), you should explore what alumni services your school has to offer. Use this, and other publications, as basic components of your own collection of career resource materials. Find books, people (counselors, librarians, family members, friends), and places (career services offices of schools near home, libraries, resource centers) that can provide both information and motivation. While you certainly should look ahead with confidence, don't be afraid to look back to analyze or reevaluate your resume, correspondence style, and efforts to date. Don't be too critical and, remember, don't place responsibility for success or failure on pieces of paper— although you may want to evaluate what you have undertaken and the tools utilized so far.

Follow up with people you haven't communicated with in a while, even if they rejected your candidacy at one time. *Liberal Arts Jobs* contains a ten-step approach to the job search. Whether you follow this brief outline or another, establish a game plan and follow it. The more structure and direction you have, the better. Although you will become tempted to become more and more "open," stay as focused as possible. Don't ignore the earlier advice concerning part-time employment. Volunteering for a while can lead to paying opportunities. Also, think about taking a course or two related to your areas of interest. This will continue to build your skills, project a commitment to a field (or fields), keep you energized, and could give you access to the career services facility of the local college or community college where you enroll. One of the key liberal arts skills, a building block of liberal arts power, is your ability to absorb and apply newly acquired knowledge quickly. Show potential employers that this is the case.

Experienced Workers Wanting to (or Forced to) Make a Change . . .

For you, as well as those you communicate with, the resume will be a symbol that you have begun the process of job search, so don't delay. Whether you have set a job search in motion by choice or because of circumstances beyond your control, don't underestimate the liberal arts power you possess or the importance of your resume. Your resume must project professionalism and maturity; it must be dynamic and bold. Networking and an ongoing flow of communications (verbal and written) will be critical to your efforts. As stated before, the more focused you are, the more liberal arts powerful you can be. This book contains some sample resumes used by experienced job seekers and discusses their efforts. Whether you are making a transition (seeking something completely different) or building upon earlier or current employment experiences, review *all* sections of this book carefully and pull out the pieces of relevant information, even if they appear to be directed toward recent graduates. In many ways you are truly the most liberal arts powerful of all job seekers: you have a proven track record of success. But you can also be the most likely to become frustrated and overcome by self-doubt. While you may have to polish your research skills a bit, and it might be wise to take a course or seminar to set you off in the right direction, you still possess the liberal arts response-ability to be a successful job seeker. Use it!

Whatever group you are in, remember that the resume is a tool. Keep in mind as you proceed that there are many ways in which you can use it to be successful.

Steps to Writing Your Resume: A Quick Overview

Working through these exercises will help you answer the questions "What do I have to offer an employer?" and "What kind of resume is best for me?"

The steps described here and detailed in following sections have been developed to help you think about your skills and write your resume in a systematic fashion. The first three steps involve reviewing and documenting your accomplishments and identifying potential job search targets. These exercises will help you answer the questions "What do I have to offer an employer?" "What can I put on my resume?" and "What specific jobs should I keep in mind when writing my resume?" Working through Steps 4 and 5 will help you find answers to the questions "What kind of resume is best for me?" "Should I write more than one resume?" and "How do I go about writing my resume and having it printed and duplicated?" Numerous liberal arts job seekers have used this method with very positive results, creating resumes that turned out to be very effective tools that helped them land the jobs they wanted.

Each step is accompanied by exercises and examples that illustrate the actions you must take to complete the step. In addition, target time frames are given for each step. These are meant to provide you with some idea of how many hours it might take to complete each task and to motivate you to allot yourself the time required to do a good job. Note that the total time suggested for completing your resume is 12 to 21 hours. This does not mean that you should accomplish everything in one day, undertaking a marathon resume-writing effort. The activities should be completed over at least a few days. There are times in the resume-writing process when you must stop and think, or simply relax, before continuing with the next step.

Proceed through the steps one by one. You can complete the steps at a more leisurely pace than the one suggested by the target time frames, but you should not procrastinate or get bogged down with trivial details. Managing your time, that is, giving yourself enough time to be successful and not wasting time, is very important. It means organizing your schedule so that you have the time you need to do a careful job.

Use the following summary and target time frames to get an idea of what is involved and to organize yourself. Before you actually begin each step, review the goals so that you are absolutely sure of what you want to accomplish at each stage.

Steps to Writing Your Resume: A Quick Overview

Step 1   The Chronological Flowchart

This exercise helps you to document your educational history, notable achievements and activities, and employment experience. You can then use this information to develop a multipurpose or targeted chronological resume. This exercise also provides a basis for Step 2, the Skills Inventory and Skills Flowchart.
Target Time: 2 to 4 hours

Step 2   The Skills Inventory and Skills Flowchart

These exercises guide you in identifying skills you possess and, specifically, those you have developed through experiences documented on the Chronological Flowchart—skills that are associated with functioning successfully on the job. Once you have a complete list of your skills, you will be able to focus more easily on specific job targets. You can use the information presented on your Skills Inventory and Skills Flowchart to create a functional resume.
Target Time: 2 to 4 hours

Step 3   The Job Target Chart

After completing this step you should be better able to identify the jobs you want to aim for and the skills you have developed that should be presented as qualifications for these jobs. You can use this information to devise targeted resumes and to prepare for employment interviews.
Target Time: 2 to 4 hours

Step 4   The Review of Sample Resumes

This step involves examining the sample resumes and accompanying analyses to identify which ones illustrate the kinds of contents and formats that would best serve your purposes. All of the resumes were written by liberal arts job seekers, and they include resumes of homemakers who are "returning" to work as well as people who are moving from one job or career field to another. The samples represent many different styles of resumes, and the analyses explain why each liberal arts job hunter developed a particular resume. Instructions on how to use the samples to develop a rough draft of your resume are also given.
Target Time: 2 to 3 hours

Step 5   Writing Your Resume

This is a process that takes you through several revisions from a rough draft to a final version of your resume. Guidelines for critiquing your drafts are presented.
Target Time: 4 to 6 hours

The Chronological Flowchart

The Chronological Flowchart enables you to identify and document your experiences and achievements in a systematic fashion.

The Chronological Flowchart is a document on which you record your educational and employment experiences and achievements in the order of their occurrence. This document will subsequently enable you to identify your skills and, ultimately, to write your resume.

Study the model that appears on pages 17 to 21, then use the formatted pages in the Appendix to prepare your own Chronological Flowchart. Before you begin, however, and before you thoroughly review the sample flowchart, let's review the individual components of the chart.

Dates. Record these in the left-hand margin. Start with the present, noting year and month, academic year, or season, and proceed in reverse chronological order, going as far back as you desire.

Educational History. Describe your graduate, undergraduate, high school, and other academic experiences. Include special programs such as foreign study and field-specific institutes (although these can also appear under the Notable Achievements and Activities heading). Cite institutions, dates attended and/or dates graduated, courses and/or majors, credits received, and as much detailed information as you deem appropriate.

Notable Achievements and Activities. Document extracurricular and community activities, travel experiences, and other achievements, including those that could appear in either of the other columns, that have given you a sense of accomplishment and that you judge to be of particular note. List the experience and describe the circumstances and accomplishments involved.

Employment History. List full-time and part-time jobs, internships, and other work experience. Cite where you worked and titles you held, and describe the nature of your activities. You can record volunteer experiences here or under Notable Achievements and Activities, depending on whether or not you see them as work experience.

Stacey York's Chronological Flowchart is presented to illustrate how your flowchart might look. To show how one can take this document to the final production of a resume, Stacey's resumes are included among the samples, on pages 95 and 96. While Stacey is a true job seeker I worked with, obviously, she is a truly exceptional individual, as exemplified by the quality and quantity of her experiences. It is because she has such a variety of accomplishments that I selected her flowchart as an illustration. Study her flowchart carefully to see the kinds of things she has included. Do not, however, compare yourself with her. You should not judge the quality of your flowchart, or your past experiences, by comparing them with the experiences of others. *You are to use this exercise to simply document your accomplishments, not to judge them!*

The more information you have on your chart, the more control you will have over the resume-writing process.

Start your chart by filling in the dates column, then complete the other sections. There is no limit to the number of pages your chart can be. Be as thorough as possible—not critical. The more information you have on your chart, the easier the subsequent steps will be and the more control you will have over the resume-writing process. Now is the time to put *everything* down; later you will be more selective about the information you actually use.

Once you have completed the first draft of your flowchart, put it down for a few hours. Then review what you have written, adding information where you feel the chart is incomplete. You may wish to have a friend, family member, or supervisor review the draft with you. Such people might remember details you have forgotten or overlooked.

When you have completed the Chronological Flowchart you may be tempted to skip the next steps and go on to write a multipurpose chronological resume. (And this may be the only way to proceed if you must have a resume quickly for the interview you have scheduled two days from now.) I strongly recommend, however, that you complete the Skills Inventory and Skills Flowchart and Job Target Chart so that you will develop more focused objectives and have the option of writing either a functional or a chronological resume. Do not be too quick to skip steps. The more thoroughly you complete all three steps, the more effective your resume, or resumes, will be and the more control you will have over the entire job-hunting process.

Chronological Flowchart   Stacey York

DATES	EDUCATIONAL HISTORY	NOTABLE ACHIEVEMENTS AND ACTIVITIES	EMPLOYMENT HISTORY
SENIOR YEAR 1989–90			
Spring Term 1990	STANFORD UNIVERSITY A.B., expected June 1990 Major: English Literature	Graduation!	
Winter Term 1990 Fall Term 1989	Courses: Fables & Fabulists, Graphic Art, English Independent Study	3.2 GPA as of Fall 1989	
		STANFORD WOMEN'S CREW Coxswain Novice Four 1988–present	STANFORD SPORTS INFORMATION OFFICE
		Editor, *STANFORD CREW NOTES* Fall 1988–present Write copy; edit and lay out monthly editions; circulate to appropriate on-campus departments and publications, off-campus publications, and alumni.	Administrative Intern Spring 1988–present Report on all sports events; manage postgame pressbox operations for football season; write articles on Stanford athletes for press releases and athletic department publications; assist in development of press guides and programs.
		PANHELLENIC SOCIETY Representative of Alpha Chi Omega Sorority Fall 1989	Football Statistician Fall 1989 and 1988 Compiled statistics; wrote game summaries and weekly reports.
		STANFORD SPORTS NEWS SAN FRANCISCO CHRONICLE SAN JOSE MERCURY NEWS THE STANFORD DAILY Fall 1986–present Write various articles on Stanford athletics.	
Summer 1989	Term Off		MOBIL OIL CORPORATION Public Relations Intern Summer 1989 Assisted staff writers in research for Mobil's Op Ed advertisements, "Observations" columns, and special publications. Proofread copy and checked facts; replied to reader correspondence; coordinated Mobil's School Visitation Program.

Chronological Flowchart   Stacey York

DATES	EDUCATIONAL HISTORY	NOTABLE ACHIEVEMENTS AND ACTIVITIES	EMPLOYMENT HISTORY
JUNIOR YEAR 1988–89			
Spring Term 1989	STANFORD IN FRANCE Spring 1989 Studied language and culture while living with French family in Nice, France, and attending the Université de Nice.	Traveled throughout France, Italy, and Germany.	
Winter Term 1989	Courses: Introductory French II, Shakespeare II, Instrument Instruction—Keyboard.	STANFORD ALUMNI CLUB OF NORTHERN NEW JERSEY Student Liaison Officer Spring 1988–Winter 1989 Coordinated activities for prospective Stanford students from northern New Jersey at Alumni Club events in NJ and at Stanford. Represented Stanford at college nights at high schools in NJ. Corresponded with applicants and alumni concerning campus events. Greeted and hosted Alumni Club members, freshmen, and prospective students during visits to campus.	
Fall Term 1988	Courses: Introductory French I, Developmental Psychology, Shakespeare I	*THE STANFORD DAILY* Sports Reporter Winter 1987–Fall 1988 Covered various sports events for student newspaper. ALPHA CHI OMEGA SORORITY Rush Cochair Fall 1988 Assisted in planning of all rush functions.	

Chronological Flowchart   Stacey York

DATES	EDUCATIONAL HISTORY	NOTABLE ACHIEVEMENTS AND ACTIVITIES	EMPLOYMENT HISTORY
Summer Term 1988	Courses: Introduction to the Theater, Contemporary American Fiction, Role of Computer Outside Science, Recent U.S. History		PALO ALTO HILTON INN Hostess and Waitress Summer 1988 part-time
SOPHOMORE YEAR 1987–1988			
Spring Term 1988	INDEPENDENT STUDY PROJECT Spring 1988 Surveyed student attitudes concerning Stanford Honor Code. Presented results in videotape presentation to student and faculty groups and to administration. Courses: Policy Studies Independent Study, Introduction to Journalism II, Art—Basic Design		STANFORD SPORTS INFORMATION OFFICE Administrative Intern Spring 1988 Selected as one of three interns from over twenty applicants.
Winter 1988	Term Off		MACY'S DEPARTMENT STORE Salesperson in "Junior World" Winter 1988 Assisted customers, maintained stock, assisted buyers in selecting merchandise.
Fall Term 1987	SOCIAL PSYCHOLOGY RESEARCH STUDY Fall 1987 Conducted survey of passengers using shuttle-bus system utilizing interviews. Developed questionnaires, collected and analyzed data to determine use patterns and opinions. Results presented to shuttle-bus management. Courses: Social Psychology, Women & Literature, Introduction to Policy Studies		

Chronological Flowchart   Stacey York

DATES	EDUCATIONAL HISTORY	NOTABLE ACHIEVEMENTS AND ACTIVITIES	EMPLOYMENT HISTORY
Summer 1987	Term Off		MACY'S DEPARTMENT STORE Salesperson in "Housewares" Summer 1987 Assisted customers and maintained stock.
FRESHMAN YEAR 1986–87			
Spring Term 1987	Courses: Instrument Instruction—Keyboard, Introduction to Psychology, American Political System	STANFORD ALUMNI CLUB OF NORTHERN NEW JERSEY Student Liaison Officer Spring 1987 Selected as one of two student liaison officers.	
Winter Term 1987	Courses: English Literature—Chaucer to Milton; Calculus and Differential Equations; Introduction to Journalism I		
Fall Term 1986	STANFORD UNIVERSITY Enrolled as freshman Courses: Introduction to Literature and Composition, History of the U.S. 1700–1900, Introduction to Calculus		
Summer 1986			MACY'S DEPARTMENT STORE Supervisor/Salesperson Fall 1984–Summer 1986 Responsible for salespersons, nightly closing activities, and maintaining departments in managers' absence. Rotated throughout store as needed. Youngest such supervisor in store. Worked evenings, weekends, and holidays.

Chronological Flowchart   Stacey York

DATES	EDUCATIONAL HISTORY	NOTABLE ACHIEVEMENTS AND ACTIVITIES	EMPLOYMENT HISTORY
SENIOR YEAR 1985–86	COLUMBIA HIGH SCHOOL Diploma, June 1986 Top 10% of class of 850	NATIONAL HONOR SOCIETY 1985 *THE MIRROR* Senior Yearbook Editor Fall 1985–Spring 1986 Coordinated activities of five editors and twenty-five staff members. Included business and production decisions, layout, copy, advertising, and photography.	
JUNIOR YEAR 1984–85		JUNIOR CLASS SECRETARY Fall 1984–Spring 1985 *THE MIRROR* Yearbook Staff Member Winter 1984–Spring 1985 Wrote pieces, assisted in layout of sports section, and sold ads.	

The Skills Inventory

On your Chronological Flowchart, you documented academic, extracurricular, and employment experiences. In order to become a successful job hunter, you must learn how to translate experiences into skills, orienting your thinking and that of employers toward your potential for the successful performance of specific tasks.

Once you are aware of your skills and how they relate to specific jobs, you can truly create a liberal arts powerful resume.

The following exercises will assist you in identifying the skills and characteristics you have that can be applied to potential job targets. Once you are aware of your skills and how they relate to specific jobs, you can truly create a liberal arts powerful resume. It will project the abilities you have to do the job and the attitude you have to succeed, and it will allow you to take effective job search actions.

The Skills Inventory is composed of 8 *Skills Realms,* 43 *Major Skills Categories,* and 177 *Actions.* To complete it, first review your Chronological Flowchart carefully. Then, check those actions on the Skills Inventory that represent skills you utilized to accomplish events on the chronological listing. At this stage do not be too analytical when selecting actions to check. Later, you will be asked to be more selective—to, first, judge those actions that, when combined, project a major skill and to, subsequently, decide which major skills are of greatest job-related importance.

Use the formatted pages in the Appendix (or photocopies if you wish to do the exercise again), but first you may wish to review Stacey York's Skills Inventory. Again, Stacey's sample appears to illustrate how an inventory of skills *might* look, not how yours *should* look, and it is meant to model how one takes the exercises in the book to the final product, a resume.

This exercise and the Skills Flowchart exercise are tied together in a summary on page 33. Please refer to that section when you have completed *both* exercises.

1. Analytical Realm

ANALYZING AND EVALUATING
- ✔ quantitative or statistical data
- ✔ services or programs
- ___ performances of groups or individuals
- ___ value of objects or services

CLASSIFYING
- ___ objects or people into categories
- ✔ status of applicants or applications

ESTIMATING AND APPRAISING
- ___ cost of services or programs
- ___ time requirements of services to be performed or programs to take place
- ___ physical space required of services or programs

- ✔ number of persons or items required for services or programs

EXAMINING
- ___ financial records
- ✔ procedures and policies
- ___ physical objects or locations

RESEARCHING
- ✔ information from libraries or written sources
- ___ information from obscure sources
- ✔ backgrounds of groups or individuals
- ___ historical information
- ✔ information from people via interviews
- ___ information from physical evidence
- ✔ information for immediate uses
- ✔ information for continued research

2. Communications Realm

BUYING
- ✔ for resale to the public
- ___ for resale to distributors or retailers
- ___ for use by organizations or for events

CORRESPONDING
- ✔ by answering inquiries by mail or phone
- ___ by initiating contact by mail or phone

DISTRIBUTING
- ___ to persons one-on-one
- ___ to places for resale

EDITING
- ___ book manuscripts
- ✔ newspaper or magazine articles

- ✔ papers, reports, or proposals
- ✔ for grammatical errors
- ✔ for style or format

INTERPRETING AND TRANSLATING
- ✔ languages
- ___ technical data into lay terms
- ___ complicated ideas into clear language

READING AND PROOFREADING
- ✔ large amounts of information quickly
- ✔ for errors or style
- ✔ to synthesize abstracts

REPRESENTING AND RECRUITING
✔ representing an organization to the public
✔ recruiting employees or volunteers
✔ promoting a point of view, soliciting funds or aid

SELLING
✔ products or ideas one-on-one
✔ products or ideas to large groups
✔ in a store
___ door-to-door
___ by phone
___ products or services in high demand
✔ products or services where demand is created

SPEAKING
✔ publicly to audiences
✔ in small groups
✔ by developing or using presentation materials

WRITING
___ copy for sales or advertising
✔ fiction
✔ essays
✔ reports or proposals
✔ journalistic copy for print or broadcast
✔ abstracts synthesized from volumes of data or other information
✔ quickly under deadline pressure
___ slowly for accuracy, style, and content

3. Creative Realm

ARRANGING AND DISPLAYING
✔ materials and equipment for a show
✔ furniture and fixtures
✔ products for sale
✔ wall or window displays
___ landscapes

DESIGNING
✔ layouts for newspapers or magazines
✔ layouts for advertising or promotional artwork
✔ brochures, flyers, or posters
✔ artwork
✔ audiovisual materials

PERFORMING
✔ in a theatrical production
✔ in a musical production
___ in a promotional demonstration

PRINTING
___ using standard equipment and processes
___ using desktop software and hardware
___ freehand or in calligraphy

SKETCHING, PAINTING, AND PHOTOGRAPHING
✔ diagrams, charts, or graphs
___ pictures of people or things
✔ illustrations for a story, idea, proposal, or report
✔ for artistic purposes
___ for advertising or promotional purposes

4. Interactive Realm

COACHING, DIRECTING, AND TUTORING
- ✔ athletic teams
- ___ theatrical productions
- ___ academic subjects

COUNSELING AND ADVISING
- ___ on personal problems
- ___ on academic issues
- ___ on financial issues
- ✔ as resource person, referring to professionals or to reference materials
- ___ groups or clubs within an academic environment

HANDLING COMPLAINTS
- ✔ by listening and responding verbally
- ✔ by listening and responding in writing
- ___ by reading and corresponding
- ✔ by taking actions
- ___ by calming tense situations

INTERVIEWING
- ___ to determine attitudes

- ✔ to gather employment information
- ✔ to collect sales or marketing data

MEETING THE PUBLIC
- ✔ by receiving and greeting
- ✔ by giving tours
- ✔ by displaying or selling products
- ✔ by conducting surveys in person
- ✔ by conducting telephone surveys

TEACHING AND TRAINING
- ___ in a classroom or academic setting
- ✔ in a recreational setting
- ✔ in a business setting
- ✔ groups
- ✔ individuals
- ___ physical activities and sports
- ___ academic subjects
- ___ self-improvement
- ___ work-related performance skills and ideas

5. Organizational Realm

MANAGING
- ✔ the performance and productivity of others
- ✔ information or data collection
- ✔ activities of groups or individuals
- ✔ by delegating tasks
- ✔ a store
- ✔ an event

PLANNING
- ✔ an event
- ___ a trip

- ✔ a system or program
- ✔ sales, advertising, or promotional activities
- ___ based on cost/benefit or financial criteria

RECORDKEEPING
- ✔ numerical data
- ✔ files and records
- ___ database systems

SUPERVISING AND OVERSEEING
- ✔ work of others

___physical plants, apartments, or buildings
✔ systems and procedures
✔ policies and programs

TIMING
___tasks to be completed in a given period
___events to begin and end as planned
___efficiency of others

UPDATING
✔ information for day-to-day use
___filing systems
___policies and procedures
✔ biographical information
___databases

6. Physical Realm

ATHLETICS
✔ performing or coaching a sport or event
___demonstrating or selling equipment
✔ planning or promoting an event
___managing business aspects

CONSTRUCTING
___houses or buildings
___mechanical or electronic devices

___objects, such as furniture, fences, or platforms

PROTECTING
___people
___objects or buildings

REPAIRING
___mechanical or electrical devices
___cars or trucks
___home or building components

7. Quantitative Realm

ACCOUNTING AND BOOKKEEPING
___maintaining financial balances
___maintaining accounts receivable and payable
✔ tracking sales revenues versus costs
___keeping records of actions or transactions versus costs

BUDGETING
___costs of projects or systems
✔ monitoring spending
___developing cost-saving techniques or plans

CALCULATING
___by hand or with a simple calculator

COMPUTING AND DATA PROCESSING
✔ using desktop computers
___using laptop computers
___using mainframes
___for simple calculations
✔ for statistical analyses
___for database management

___using packaged
software
___writing software and
programming
___explaining hardware or
software to others

8. Scientific Realm

LABORATORY AND
MEDICAL WORK
___setting up equipment
or instruments
___using equipment or
instruments
___designing controlled
experiments
___caring for laboratory
animals
___handling specimens
___inspecting objects or
specimens

___examining people or
animals

MEASURING
___to obtain accurate
readings from devices
___to assess skills or
conditions

TREATING AND
DIAGNOSING
___animals
___humans

Summary of Skills Inventory Findings. Below are listed fifteen actions that are most job related—those Stacey would like to utilize most within the performance of day-to-day job functions and those she believes contributed most to her past achievements.

ANALYZING SERVICES OR PROGRAMS

RESEARCHING INFO FROM LIBRARIES OR WRITTEN SOURCES

RESEARCHING INFO FROM PEOPLE VIA INTERVIEWS

EDITING NEWSPAPER OR MAGAZINE NOTICES

EDITING PAPERS, REPORTS, OR PROPOSALS

REPRESENTING AN ORGANIZATION TO THE PUBLIC

PROMOTING A POINT OF VIEW

SELLING PRODUCTS OR IDEAS ONE-ON-ONE

SELLING PRODUCTS OR IDEAS TO LARGE GROUPS

WRITING EXPOSITORY MATERIAL

WRITING REPORTS OR PROPOSALS

WRITING JOURNALISTIC COPY

DESIGNING LAYOUTS FOR MAGAZINES OR NEWSPAPERS

MANAGING ACTIVITIES OF GROUPS OR INDIVIDUALS

SUPERVISING POLICIES OR PROGRAMS

These are the nine Major Skills that Stacey judges most job related and that she believes will contribute most to future achievements.

EDITING

WRITING

DESIGNING

MANAGING

MEETING THE PUBLIC

PLANNING

SELLING

RESEARCHING

REPRESENTING AND RECRUITING

The Skills Flowchart

The Skills Flowchart builds upon the information garnered from the Skills Inventory. As before, you may use the formatted pages in the Appendix (or photocopies if you wish to do the exercise again), but first you may wish to review the sample that follows on pages 31 and 32. This flowchart is composed of three components.

Be creative and open-minded when citing skills and actions associated with your experiences. Think of what you did beyond the job description.

Experience. You can list all of the academic, extracurricular, and employment experiences noted on your Chronological Flowchart or just a few, but the more you include, the more complete your skills analysis will be. You will decide later which skills you would most like to use day after day on the job through an analysis of the results of this exercise and a comparison with those of the Skills Inventory. (See page 33.)

Basic Skills and Actions. List all the skills you utilized or developed in each of your academic, extracurricular, and employment experiences. Here you are answering the basic questions "What did I do and what did I learn in connection with the job, extracurricular activity, or academic experience?" Use your Skills Inventory findings to help you identify skills and actions, but don't limit yourself to those. Be creative and open-minded when citing skills and actions associated with your experiences, and use descriptive phrasing if that helps. Think of what you did beyond the job description. For example, you might have been hired as a file clerk, but if you reorganized the filing system, you did more than merely file. Note as many skills and actions as you like, even if you did not check them off in the Skills Inventory.

Skills Headings. Next take stock of the various skills and actions you cited in the previous column and group them into a number of broad working categories, using the Major Skills Categories of the Skills Inventory if you wish. Don't, however, limit yourself to these forty-three headings. In selecting skills you want to emphasize on your resume (as well as in your job search correspondence and in your interviews), give first priority to those you enjoy using and second priority to those you think you are best at. While these are often the same, they can be different. Document your experiences under each skills heading, noting where you exercised or developed that skill.

In selecting the skills you want to emphasize on your resume, give first priority to those you enjoy using.

As you by now expect, the Skills Flowchart on pages 31 and 32 is Stacey York's, the same liberal arts job seeker whose Chronological Flowchart and Skills Inventory you have studied. By reviewing Stacey's exercises you will better understand the relationship between these three documents, the exercises that produced them, and the resumes that appear on pages 95 and 96.

You can now complete your own Skills Flowchart. Start by listing experiences from your Chronological Flowchart, then complete the other sections. As before, be thorough and list as many experiences as you wish. There is no limit to the number of entries. Again, the more information you have on your chart, the more control you will have over the resume-writing process.

Once you have completed the first draft of your Skills Flowchart, put it down for a few hours. Then review it and add to it where the information seems incomplete. As with the Chronological Flowchart, you may wish to have someone who knows you well review the draft with you.

You should spend time thinking hard about the Skills Headings section of the flowchart. When revising your initial draft, after reviewing the Major Skills Categories of the inventory, add more skills and elaborate on the situations in which you developed and used these abilities.

Skills Flowchart   Stacey York

EXPERIENCE	BASIC SKILLS AND ACTIONS	SKILLS HEADINGS
STANFORD WOMEN'S CREW	Coxswain: motivating, organizing, disciplining. Editor, *STANFORD CREW NOTES*: writing, editing, layout, circulating, promoting.	Note: Create Skills Headings by grouping the information listed under Basic Skills and Actions into several broad working categories. You can use Major Skills Categories appearing in the Skills Inventory as well as others. Once completed, these can appear as general headings for functional resumes or functional components of combination resumes.
PANHELLENIC SOCIETY	Representative: analyzing, organizing, planning, leading, decision making.	• WRITING—journalistic and expository, through course work in English and journalism and experiences with *Stanford Daily, Crew Notes,* Sports Information Office, and *The Mirror.*
STANFORD SPORTS NEWS *SAN FRANCISCO CHRONICLE* *SAN JOSE MERCURY NEWS* *THE STANFORD DAILY*	Reporter: writing, reporting, interviewing, researching.	• EDITING—knowledge of grammar and of editing through course work in English and journalism and experiences with *Stanford Daily, Crew Notes,* Sports Information Office, Mobil, and *The Mirror.*
STANFORD SPORTS INFORMATION OFFICE	Administrative Intern: writing, editing, layout, public relations, promoting. Football Statistician: calculating, analyzing, writing.	• LAYOUT AND DESIGN—knowledge of layout and design from courses in journalism and art, experiences with *Crew Notes,* Sports Information Office, *The Mirror,* and an interest in oil and acrylic painting. Also photography.
MOBIL OIL CORPORATION	Public Relations Intern: researching, proofreading, organizing, corresponding.	• RESEARCHING—learned how to develop and implement research designs by working on honor code and shuttle-bus surveys. Did research for Sports Information Office, for Mobil, and for all reporting positions.
STANFORD IN FRANCE	Traveling, learning foreign language, understanding and adapting to foreign culture, interpreting and translating.	• ORGANIZING AND MANAGING—learned how to manage tasks and people and analyze data through experiences with Macy's, Mobil, Sports Information Office, and Alpha Chi Omega Sorority.
STANFORD ALUMNI CLUB OF NORTHERN NEW JERSEY	Student Liaison Officer: organizing, representing, recruiting, promoting, public relations, corresponding.	• PERFORMING AND CREATING—knowledge of theater gained by taking courses and working on high school productions. Capable of making presentations and performing before groups. Play piano and organ; paint in watercolors.
THE STANFORD DAILY	Reporter: writing, reporting, interviewing, researching.	
ALPHA CHI OMEGA SORORITY	Rush Cochair: organizing, promoting, motivating, planning.	
INDEPENDENT STUDY PROJECT FOR POLICY STUDIES	Researching, developing surveys, interviewing, analyzing data, producing videotape presentation.	
SOCIAL PSYCHOLOGY RESEARCH STUDY	Researching, developing attitude assessment procedures, interviewing, analyzing data.	

Skills Flowchart   Stacey York

EXPERIENCE	BASIC SKILLS AND ACTIONS	SKILLS HEADINGS
PALO ALTO HILTON	Hostess and Waitress: dealing with public, handling complaints, serving public, using physical stamina on the job.	Note: Create Skills Headings by grouping the information listed under Basic Skills and Actions into several broad working categories. You can use Major Skills Categories appearing in the Skills Inventory as well as others. Once completed, these can appear as general headings for functional resumes or functional components of combination resumes.
MACY'S DEPARTMENT STORE	Salesperson: selling, buying, organizing, arranging, displaying.	
	Supervisor: supervising, organizing, motivating, selling, buying, arranging, displaying, accounting.	• PUBLIC RELATIONS AND SELLING— able to promote image and sell products (Stanford Alumni Club of Northern New Jersey, Macy's, Alpha Chi Omega Sorority, and high school yearbook experiences).
ENGLISH LITERATURE MAJOR AND JOURNAL-ISM CLASSES	Reading, writing, reporting, judging relative merits of written works, knowledge of grammar.	• FOREIGN LANGUAGE AND CULTURE— knowledge of foreign cultures gained through travel experiences and foreign study; conversant in French.
INSTRUMENTAL INSTRUCTION AND ART CLASSES	Piano playing, sketching, painting, performing.	
THE MIRROR—HIGH SCHOOL YEARBOOK	Senior Editor: editing, writing, layout, managing, delegating, motivating, photography, selling.	
	Staffer: writing, layout, photography, selling.	

Summary of the Skills Inventory and the Skills Flowchart

Now that you have inventoried skills and connected them directly to past experiences, let's analyze these two exercises and determine if any significant conclusions can be drawn. Compare your listing of Basic Skills and Actions as cited in the flowchart to your listing of the fifteen most job-related actions noted in the Summary of Skills Inventory Findings (page 28). By doing so, can you now identify a listing of the ten most job-related and experience-tested skills and actions? Note these ten liberal arts powerful skills and actions here.

_____

_____

_____

_____

_____

_____

_____

_____

_____

_____

Now compare your listings of Skills Headings in the flowchart to the nine Major Skills from the Summary of Skills Inventory Findings (page 28). Are all included? If not, which are missing and why? Did obvious patterns appear? Through this comparison, reduce the list of nine to the six most significant basic skills headings and note them here.

_____

_____

_____

_____

_____

_____

The above summary *can* be used to develop a functional resume and *should* be used to highlight your liberal arts power whenever necessary. Your liberal arts abilities of research and analysis have brought you to this point. Soon your communications skills will be used to develop your resume. Ultimately, you will use these same skills to correspond and interview with potential employers. Once you have completed the Chronological Flowchart, Skills Inventory, and Skills Flowchart, you can write a multipurpose functional resume or a simple chronological version. But, again, I strongly recommend that you complete Step 3, the Job Target Chart, so that you don't deprive yourself of the option of creating a targeted resume. By completing all exercises you will prove to yourself that the liberal arts skills you possess can be used for critical pre-search purposes as well as for job search actions.

Job Targeting

As I said at the beginning of this book, it is extremely important for you to realize that your major in college does not limit your career opportunities. Your choice of jobs will be limited only by a lack of awareness of the skills you possess and ignorance of the opportunities that exist.

Once you have identified your skills and researched the functions involved in various jobs and careers, you will know what jobs you most want to seek and you will be able to write a targeted resume. Again, true liberal arts power involves the use of research and analytical skills to uncover significant job-related abilities and to identify realistic job search goals. In addition, you must apply communication and interpersonal skills to effectively present your goals, motivation, and qualifications through resumes, correspondence, and interviews. Liberal arts power, like a beam of light, is most useful when it is focused. As I have said before, a targeted resume can be an especially effective tool for the liberal arts job seeker who wants to present himself or herself as an individual qualified to perform *on the job*. The objective you state on your resume can be a handle you can hold on to as well as a handle you can present to potential employers so they can grasp what you are looking for and the qualifications you possess. Job search can be a hazy process at best, but if you apply the brightness of a liberal arts powerful resume and job search perspective to specific targets, all can see more clearly.

Some of you have already undertaken a great deal of research and have very focused objectives in mind. If you feel you have enough information, you can go ahead and complete the Job Target Chart. If you do not have goals that you can articulate to employers, you should take a bit of time out for some research. Understanding jobs and careers is essential to developing objectives and selling your liberal arts power, and you should take the time to do the necessary research. (See "Informational Interviews: An Effective Research Technique" on pages 36 and 37.)

A good way to begin your research is to consult *Liberal Arts Jobs,* the companion to this book, as well as other resources that provide information on careers. *Liberal Arts Jobs* will show you how to begin the task of goal setting, through structured exercises, realistic perspectives, and information about more than 300 job search and career options. This book addresses the responsibility as well as the response-ability of liberal arts majors to identify not only the career fields they wish to enter but also the qualifications they need to perform job functions associated with entry-level opportunities. It provides the liberal arts major with a "term-paper perspective" as a way to effectively set job-related goals. The bibliography on page 147 of this book, the same one that appears in *Liberal Arts Jobs,* lists some of the basic materials you should be

> **Your choice of jobs will be limited only by a lack of awareness of the skills you possess and ignorance of the opportunities that exist.**

Informational Interviews: An Effective Research Technique

One of the best ways to learn about careers you are interested in is to talk with people working in those fields. Use the contacts you have now—friends, relatives, professors, alumni, and career service professionals—to help you identify likely candidates for such "informational interviews."

Tips on the informational interview:
Try to conduct your first informational interviews with people you know so you can become polished before you interview strangers.

Be thoroughly prepared. This is your show. You are conducting the interview, so feel free to use a list of prepared questions and to take notes or, if given permission, tape the session.

Always take a resume with you, even if it is a multipurpose one. You can use it to simply and quickly share information about your background so that you can get to the task of finding out about the interviewee's background more easily.

Stress that you are seeking information only, not a job. You may have to restate this several times. Honesty in this regard is very important. If after an informational interview you decide that you would like to seek employment within the organization of the interviewee, you may send a letter indicating your interest in pursuing employment and requesting information about procedures you should follow. Enclose a resume with this letter (a resume that may now have a statement of objective based on what you learned from the informational interview) and follow up with a phone call to discuss appropriate next steps.

Keep an open mind and listen closely to what is being said. Evaluate the source of the information objectively, and get more than one side of a story before deciding to stop researching a potential career or before targeting a specific job.

Always end an informational interview with a referral request, asking about other people to talk to or materials to read. In this way, you will be continually developing a network of contacts and a bibliography of resources.

Always follow up an interview with a thank-you letter. You may use the thank-you letter to request additional information or, as discussed, to ask to be considered for employment.

Questions you may wish to ask:

What are the duties/functions/responsibilities of your job?

What are the educational/training requirements?

What abilities or personal qualities do you believe are most important for this field/job?

Which of my abilities or personal qualities would be important in this field/job? (Ask this if the interviewee knows you well.)

Who is the department head or supervisor for this job? What is his/her title?

How does one enter this field/job? How did you enter it? What are typical entry-level titles and functions?

How did you get to where you are and what are your long-range goals?

Do you have any advice for someone who is trying to get started in this field?

What kind of organizations hire people to perform the functions you do here?

Do you know of other persons I may contact to discuss this career field? Can you suggest materials I should read concerning the field? (a question that should always be asked)

The more people you talk to about your career interests and about your job search efforts, the more likely you will be to succeed. If you cannot arrange an employment interview with an employer, ask for an informational interview. Keep your lines of communication open.

aware of. *Where to Start Career Planning* (distributed by Peterson's) also offers a detailed listing of valuable resources. Remember, you don't have to stop the resume process to undertake and complete your goal setting. Multipurpose resumes are appropriate as first editions, with subsequent, more targeted resumes indicating greater liberal arts power. Don't ignore the critical research phase of the job search process, but don't, on the other hand, use it as an excuse to delay completion of your resume.

The more you know about a career field and your job target, the more likely you will be to receive an offer to work within that field.

The information you acquire through reading and informational interviews, added to what you already know about career fields and what you will learn from other sources, will help you focus your thinking and decide on job goals. And once you establish your goals you will be prepared to write an effective resume and take appropriate action. Remember, the more you know about a career field and your job target, the more likely you will be to receive an offer to work within that field. Liberal arts graduates who have not had course work or experiences that are directly related to a specific industry must show that they are knowledgeable about the jobs they are seeking. You must apply your most basic liberal arts skills, those of research, analysis, and communication, to the critical tasks of setting goals and focusing your liberal arts power.

Your Job Target Chart will bring together the information from your Chronological Flowchart, Skills Inventory, and Skills Flowchart as well as the results of your research into jobs and careers, showing how your experiences relate to jobs you are interested in. If you have read *Liberal Arts Jobs* and completed the Job Search Matrix, this exercise will simply be a matter of reformatting information already available. If you have not, but you have utilized other resources to research options, you can complete this exercise without too much difficulty. Be as thorough as possible. There is no limit to the number of pages your chart can be. Again, the more information you put on the chart, the easier subsequent steps will be.

First review the sample, created by Stacey York, on pages 41 and 42. To complete your Job Target Chart, you may, as with all other exercises in this book, use the formatted pages appearing in the Appendix. If you don't wish to use the formatted pages, you can make several three-column sheets with the headings appearing on the sample and in the order discussed below.

If you have a clear understanding of what is expected of someone who holds a particular job, you will be able to communicate your goals and qualifications to employers.

Field/Job Title. List the career fields and job titles that interest you most. Do not be afraid to state specific titles. By doing so you are not "limiting yourself" or "closing any doors," phrases I hear too often from liberal arts job seekers who in fact limit themselves by their lack of focus and who have trouble finding a job because they are unwilling to open doors. You are not accepting a job offer here, but simply stating potential job targets. If you are unable to come up with titles you are interested in, perhaps you should undertake a bit more career research.

Functional Description. For each career field and job you have listed as a potential job target in the first column, describe in concise terms the functions and day-to-day responsibilities. Quantity—the length of your description—is less important than quality. If you have a clear understanding of what is expected of someone who holds a particular job, and if you are able to write accurate descriptions of potential job targets, you are prepared to communicate your goals and qualifications to a potential employer. You are then ready to sell your liberal arts power. If you are unable to articulate your job goals, you must continue your exploration of careers by reading appropriate materials and interviewing people who are knowledgeable.

Relevant Experiences, Skills, and Interview Linkages. In the last column of this chart, you relate to your potential job targets the information contained in previous exercises. The Chronological Flowchart documents the experiences that have given you opportunities to develop and utilize skills. The Skills Inventory and Skills Flowchart identified and described skills you wish to use on the job. Now, using all three, cite the experiences and skills that relate to the *functions* of each job you cited in the Field/Job Title column.

> **Understanding job requirements and being able to make the connection between what the job demands and what you can offer is crucial to success in the job hunt.**

In the process of matching up your skills and specific job functions, you may find that you need to rewrite your brief descriptions of your experiences and abilities in order to tailor them to your job targets. This is where "selling yourself" comes in. *The more you can make your qualifications fit the job description, the more qualified for the job you can appear!* I am not talking about distorting the truth or making up false information. I am saying that you need to know about specific job requirements and you need to be able to show how your skills and knowledge are appropriate for jobs you are interested in. This is crucial to success in your job hunt. It is not puffing up your credentials or proving that you're the best. It is simply making the connection between what you can offer and what the job demands. Making this connection between your past and present self and your future working self through research, analysis, and imagination is what liberal arts power is all about. In fact, to start you on the way to using your liberal arts power in the employment interview process, this exercise also asks you to cite a few "interview linkages" for each of the fields and jobs noted. An interview linkage is simply a point of reference from which you can build a descriptive bridge from your past to your future—the targeted job. As you can see from Stacey's sample, a linkage is either a significant accomplishment, an anecdote, or an example of how skills were used to accomplish goals. Note at least two for each field/job, but don't *limit* yourself to this number. Additional information on interviewing appears later in this book, and you will see how you can use some of these linkages to complete the Pre-Interview Resume Exercise.

Once you have completed the first draft of your Job Target Chart, put it down for at least a few hours. Then review it to see whether you need to add information to it; you may see that you don't have enough information about a particular career and that you need to do additional research. You may wish to have a career counselor, friend, family member, or someone working in a career field of interest (perhaps someone you have interviewed for information) review the draft with you. His or her reactions could be very valuable. You may also want to actually draw up your resume before undertaking additional research. Knowing where you are going—what your resume might look like and how you might use it as part of an effective job-hunting campaign—could provide necessary direction to your research.

Remember, be thorough! It may take more than one draft to complete the Job Target Chart exercise. Do not be afraid to take some time out to continue exploring careers before you go on to the next resume-writing steps. After completing the final draft of your Job Target Chart, pick the three job titles from the Field/Job Title column that are of most interest to you. You may use these three potential job targets as objectives on three separately targeted resumes or, if they are related to each other, incorporate them on a single targeted resume. The limit of three does not mean that you cannot look for jobs other than those listed, but it does help you set priorities and cope with a manageable number of goals.

Having completed the first three of the five steps outlined on page 14, you are now prepared to write a multipurpose or targeted resume, using either a functional or chronological format. You can now move on to the final steps, which involve reviewing samples and analyses, writing drafts and a final version, and printing and duplication.

Keep in mind that you can go back and revise your charts or begin anew at any time. Remember, your first resume will not be your last!

READ ON . . . IDENTIFY RESUMES THAT CAN BE USED FOR YOUR PURPOSES . . . PUT YOUR LIBERAL ARTS POWER ON PAPER . . . WRITE AN EFFECTIVE RESUME AND SUCCEED!!

Job Target Chart   Stacey York

Page 1

FIELD/JOB TITLE	FUNCTIONAL DESCRIPTION	RELEVANT EXPERIENCES, SKILLS, AND INTERVIEW LINKAGES
PRINT & BROADCAST MEDIA—JOURNALISM • Editorial Assistant • Researcher • Reporter	**EDITORIAL ASSISTANT** (working for newspapers, magazines, or book publishers; assisting editors with activities involved in the preparation of copy, photography, illustration and graphics). Develop and assign story ideas; communicate with writers and readers; proof, edit, and rewrite copy; lay out publications; coordinate printing activities; and attend to details involved in all areas of editing and publishing. **RESEARCHER** (working for newspapers or magazines or radio or television stations). Research specific story-related facts to develop story and to check accuracy of story; maintain files on subject areas, including facts and photographs; provide writers and reporters with information as needed; proof, edit, and rewrite copy; locate hard-to-find information when needed. **REPORTER** (working for newspapers or magazines or radio or television stations). Research and write stories. Direct writing and reporting style to particular audience.	**EXPERIENCES** • *Stanford Daily* • *Crew Notes* • Sports Information Office • Mobil Corporation • English and Journalism Courses • Free-Lance Articles • *The Mirror* **SKILLS** • Writing • Editing • Layout and Design • Researching • Organizing and Managing • Performing **INTERVIEW LINKAGES** • Portfolio shows a depth of knowledge and experience for sports but breadth related to other areas. Discuss three articles that I'm most proud of, explaining how assignment came about and how I handled researching and writing pieces. • Independent Study of Honor Code demonstrates abilities to take relevant question and transform it into research undertaking and "broadcast" findings through mixed media.
ADVERTISING • Account Executive Trainee • Media Planner • Market Researcher	**ACCOUNT EXECUTIVE TRAINEE** (working for advertising agencies as a trainee, as an entry-level employee in media planning or market research, or as an assistant account executive). Account executives coordinate all who work on the ad campaign, interacting with client and agency personnel. Account executives utilize marketing and financial analysis skills to make decisions concerning ad campaigns. **ENTRY-LEVEL MEDIA PLANNER** (determining which types of media are most cost-effective for meeting desired goals of ad campaigns and undertaking administrative tasks associated with purchasing advertising time or space). Media planners use quantitative abilities to determine appropriate media for campaign and to write contracts. Media planners must learn about various types of media, their costs, and their influence on target markets and maintain awareness of changing media trends. **MARKET RESEARCHER** (compiling and analyzing data to plan campaigns). Market researchers also develop and administer surveys, conduct market group discussions, and utilize data-collection techniques to analyze motivation and buying behavior and to determine effectiveness of campaigns.	**EXPERIENCES** • Sports Information Office • Independent Study Project • Social Psychology Research Project • Alpha Chi Omega Sorority • Stanford Alumni Club of Northern New Jersey • Macy's Department Store Note: It may become obvious when a list of experiences becomes rather long that you are *very* qualified for a particular job and that a functional or combination resume, highlighting skills associated with the experiences, would be effective. **SKILLS** • Organizing and Managing • Researching • Layout and Design • Public Relations and Selling • Creating **INTERVIEW LINKAGES** • Special Back-to-School promotional event for Macy's. Discuss the idea and how I sold it to my superiors and the contributions I made to its success. • Sociology and Independent Studies, as well as Sports Information undertakings, involved direct application of attitudinal research. Understanding of reality-based view of research and analysis, not just theoretical.

Job Target Chart   Stacey York

FIELD/JOB TITLE	FUNCTIONAL DESCRIPTION	RELEVANT EXPERIENCES, SKILLS, AND INTERVIEW LINKAGES
CONSULTING • Research Assistant or Associate	**RESEARCH ASSISTANT/ASSOCIATE** (working for general management, strategic planning, or specialized consulting firms). Research may involve large industry overviews or specialized analyses concerning particular issues. Information gathered is used by consultants to determine possible solution to clients' problems and to develop reports and presentations to make to clients.	**EXPERIENCES** • Independent Study Project • Social Psychology Research Project • English Literature Major • Psychology Minor **SKILLS** • Researching • Writing • Organizing and Managing **INTERVIEW LINKAGES** • Mobil experience created a desire to understand complexities of business problems, to use research to identify options and solutions, and to succeed in this environment. • Ability to research, analyze, and communicate was cornerstone for numerous academic, extracurricular, and employment successes. Especially: Mobil, Sports Information, Sociology and Independent Studies, and research-oriented course work.
POLITICS • Aide for candidate or officeholder	**POLITICAL AIDE.** This work involves assisting in campaign efforts or in daily operations of offices, coordinating volunteers, arranging for press coverage of events, acting as an advance person to coordinate all aspects of visit or event, and researching possible policy position papers. Operations work involves communicating with constituents, researching potential legislation and related issues, developing draft legislation and policy statements, and writing press releases for officeholder.	**EXPERIENCES** • Stanford Alumni Club of Northern New Jersey • Independent Study Project • Social Psychology Research Project • Macy's Department Store • Alpha Chi Omega Sorority • Panhellenic Society • Stanford Sports Information Office • English Literature Major • Psychology Minor **SKILLS** • Organizing and Managing • Public Relations and Selling • Researching • Writing **INTERVIEW LINKAGES** • Mobil experience made me aware of the power of communications and the influence of public policy on corporate issues and, therefore, people's lives. • Interactions with Stanford Alumni Club provided exposure to people of various backgrounds, including officeholders, and made me aware of the impact one person can have on recruiting and fund-raising programs. One person can have impact on campaign or office operations.

Sample Resumes

Now that you have established potential job targets, you are prepared to undertake the next step toward completion of your resume: the review of sample resumes and identification of styles and formats that best serve your purposes. The sample resumes presented for your review were written by liberal arts graduates with a variety of backgrounds and career goals, and they illustrate different formats and duplication techniques. The three most basic formats—chronological, functional, and combination—are represented.

You are now prepared to undertake the next step toward completion of your resume: the review of sample resumes and identification of styles and formats that best serve your purposes.

To review: The *chronological* resume is the most traditional format, with information presented under major headings in reverse chronological order. The *functional* resume is skills oriented, presenting information under skills headings and describing experiences in terms of the functions performed. The *combination* resume is a blend of these formats. Some of the resumes were written with a specific job objective in mind, while others were developed to be used for exploring a variety of career possibilities.

Each sample resume is accompanied by a discussion of the resume writer's particular situation and reasons for using a certain approach. These analyses give you an insider's perspective, showing you the problems liberal arts resume writers confront and the way they can solve them by using creative formats, graphics, and copying techniques.

New in this edition are discussions of the job search efforts of selected resume writers. Projecting my belief in the power of a well-written resume, I have entitled these discussions "Job Search Success Stories." These appear, in their own section, directly following all the sample resumes.

Remember, no matter how well written, how powerful, your resume is, it is only a tool and must be used effectively. Whatever your abilities and attitudes, a liberal arts powerful resume cannot be completely effective without your taking powerful actions.

To determine which liberal arts job seekers share background characteristics—majors, extracurriculars, work experiences—with you, ask yourself the following questions after you have completed your first perusal of the samples and analyses.

Which resumes state career goals that are of interest to me?

Which resumes contain descriptions of academic, extracurricular, and work experiences that seem to parallel mine?

Which resumes do I find most attractive and why?

Which design and duplication techniques seem most effective?

Which formats would be most appropriate for my purposes?

Which analyses discuss circumstances similar to my own?

Which resumes are the best models for me?

The resumes presented here document real academic, extracurricular, and work experiences.

There is nothing more frustrating for a liberal arts resume writer than to review sample resumes that seem to be written by super students, resumes that describe accomplishments that seem beyond the capabilities of most students. The resumes presented here document real academic, extracurricular, and work experiences. Although the names of students, schools, and employers have been changed to ensure confidentiality, most of the resumes presented in the following pages are of actual liberal arts job seekers who landed good jobs after graduation. Moreover, most of the sample resumes have been reviewed by employers from different industries to ensure that they reflect the qualities employers seek.

Review the samples and analyses with an open mind. Avoid making statements like "Look at all he has done! I haven't done anything." "She is interested in banking and has worked in a bank for three summers. I don't have any related work experience." "How can I compete with people whose resumes look like this?" *The samples are meant to help you write the very best resume possible, not to frustrate you.* They are presented to illustrate various approaches to resume writing, so do not compare yourself to these liberal arts resume writers. Each job seeker is an individual, and you will be successful with your own background and qualifications.

As I have addressed in earlier sections and through earlier exercises, *the key to success—the basis of your liberal arts power— is your review of past experiences, identification of skills, and use of these skills in a goal-directed fashion as qualifications for particular jobs.* You are able to complete this process effectively because of what your liberal arts education has provided. *Your abilities, attitude, and actions will allow you to write your own job search success stories,* and I am confident that your resume will be, in time, as impressive as any that follow.

Jordan Elizabeth Alna:
This Biology Major Means Business

Special Features
- A combination functional and chronological resume using a Qualifications and Capabilities section
- Creative graphics highlight headings

The Problem. Jordan Elizabeth Alna wanted to stress the fact that she had diverse interests and abilities. She had not only a science major but numerous work and extracurricular experiences as well, and each of these experiences had provided her with skills that she believed could be presented as qualifications to an employer in the business world.

Jordan had at first thought it would be best to use a traditional chronological resume to present and describe her diverse experiences. After trying this kind of resume out on several employers without success, however, she was told by a helpful recruiter that even though the word "business" was included in the objective, the resume gave the impression that Jordan was interested primarily in lab research. This was because she had emphasized her biology training at the beginning of the resume.

The Solution. After mulling over the recruiter's comments, Jordan thought it might be best to try out a combination functional and chronological resume. She decided that the first thing she needed to do was specify a narrower job target. After realizing that she was more interested in the health-care industry than in business in general, *Jordan chose to focus on jobs in the areas of pharmaceutical sales, health-care administration, and public relations for hospitals or health-care products manufacturers.* She then added a Qualifications and Capabilities section in which she presented, in order of greatest significance, a summary of accomplishments that reflect skills required in the stated Objective. Jordan's revised resume, one that better matched the skills and interests stated in her Objective, turned out to be much more dynamic than her chronological version in its presentation of the specific skills that can be used on the job.

Special Note. *In addition to investigating the options discussed above, Jordan is exploring the possibilities of teaching science courses in a private secondary school or of obtaining a position in a residence life office of a college or university.* For these positions, Jordan developed a separate chronological resume without an Objective. For these fields, the more detailed chronological approach was more appropriate.

Format and Layout. Jordan's resume features very appealing graphics. The spacing is attractive, and the double rules to the left and right of each heading clearly set off one section from another. Jordan also made use of several different techniques to highlight important words—larger type and capital letters for main headings, italics for degrees and titles, and bold for significant entries in the Qualifications and Capabilities section.

Summary. Jordan the biology major means business. She first tried out a chronological resume, believing it would be the most effective type for her to use, but she had the courage to change the resume to create a better job search tool. Jordan the biology major transfused her resume and entire job search with additional liberal arts power.

See Jordan's job search success story on page 97.

JORDAN ELIZABETH ALNA

Doane Hall, Box A11
Denison University
Granville, Ohio 43023
614-587-6276

34 Glenmere Road
Little Rock, Arkansas 72116
501-753-0055

OBJECTIVE

Opportunity to use organizational and communications skills and scientific background in the health-care industry.

QUALIFICATIONS AND CAPABILITIES

As Management Intern and Office Assistant worked within business settings requiring public relations and organizational abilities. Coordinated activities and interacted with the public. Capable of creating and implementing plans and organizing resources and personnel to meet objectives.

Extracurricular activities and work experiences involved establishment of personal and group goals, development of plans for accomplishing specific tasks, management of procedures and personnel, and use of persuasive skills.

As Hospital Volunteer was exposed to all operations of health-care facility and worked with doctors, nurses, administrators, and volunteers.

Academic course work in natural sciences provided understanding of scientific method, laboratory experience, and knowledge of theories and applications.

As Teaching Assistant developed lesson plans and acted as a liaison between professor and students. Capable of making group presentations and evaluating performance of others.

As Research Assistant followed instructions and worked independently, maintaining accurate records and writing detailed reports. Capable of working without supervision.

As Resident Adviser trained in counseling and program planning. Capable of motivating others to accomplish objectives and dealing with problem situations.

EDUCATION

DENISON UNIVERSITY
Bachelor of Science in Biology

Granville, Ohio
May 1990

WORK EXPERIENCE

DENISON UNIVERSITY DEPARTMENT OF BIOLOGY
Teaching Assistant
Research Assistant

Granville, Ohio
Fall 1989 and Spring 1990
Spring 1989–Spring 1990

DENISON UNIVERSITY OFFICE OF RESIDENCE LIFE
Resident Adviser

Granville, Ohio
Fall 1988–Spring 1990

DENISON UNIVERSITY OFFICE OF HOUSING AND CONFERENCE COORDINATION
Management Intern
Coordinated conferences and programs. Arranged for facilities and equipment.
Planned housing assignments.
Represented Denison at social functions. Compiled and analyzed evaluations
and wrote report suggesting improvements.

Granville, Ohio
Summer 1989

MERRILL LYNCH
Office Assistant
Answered customer questions by phone and performed secretarial functions
for Financial Consultants.

Little Rock, Arkansas
Summer 1988

EXTRACURRICULAR ACTIVITIES

KAPPA KAPPA GAMMA SORORITY
Panhellenic Rush Chairperson
Elected to coordinate rush activities of all sororities. Designed and prepared
rush booklet. Organized pre-rush activities.
Member

Denison University
Fall 1989–Spring 1990

Spring 1987–Spring 1990

SOPHOMORE ADVISERS
Sophomore Adviser Coordinator
Elected to coordinate social functions and promote group unity. Established
newsletter. Organized retreat.
Represented sophomore advisers to administration.

Denison University
Spring 1988

MEMORIAL HOSPITAL
Volunteer

North Little Rock, Arkansas
Summers 1986 and 1987

REFERENCES

Available upon request.

Joseph E. Byrne:
An Anthropology Major
Discovers the Law

Special Features
- Targeted resume with skills noted in the statement of Objective
- Simple resume highlighting accomplishments

The Problem. From the day he entered college, Joseph E. Byrne thought that he wanted to pursue a career in retailing someday. He did not know that he would major in anthropology and minor in psychology, nor that he would grow more and more interested in law as a career field as he got closer to graduation. In fact, during his senior year *Joe decided that he would postpone his plans for a retailing career in order to explore law-related jobs.* "I have so much retail and sales experience, I could always get into retailing if I wanted to," he told himself. He felt that working for a law firm for a year or two would help him decide whether law school was the right next step. After talking to several alumni and to counselors at his college's career planning and placement office, Joe developed a resume that he could use in his efforts to find such a position. The problem Joe had to overcome was that he had taken no law-related course work and had no law-related work experience.

The Solution. Joe decided that the best way to sell his strengths would be to simply state on the resume the two most important qualities he possesses that are important in law-related jobs—research and writing skills. He includes these skills in his Objective and supports his claim of possessing them in the discussion of skills that follows.

Joe presents all of his academic and employment experiences in a straightforward and traditional manner, highlighting certain employment accomplishments by indenting the explanations. His resume thus combines the functional and chronological approaches.

Joe also uses several writing samples as evidence of his skills. He summarizes some of his best research papers and creates a collection of abstracts to distribute to potential employers. These abstracts note the varied research topics Joe undertook while in school and illustrate his writing style. *Of course, Joe makes a connection between his academic experiences and the requirements of working for a law firm in his cover letters.* (See samples beginning on page 134.)

Format and Layout. Joe's resume is traditional in its appearance because most law firms are traditional and somewhat conservative. He wanted to make the very best first impression by using a resume that is well written and professionally printed.

Summary. Joe discovered late in his academic career that he wanted to explore law as a possible profession, and he has decided to do so by taking a job in the field. This simple yet effective resume is his first step to success.

See Joe's job search success story on page 98.

JOSEPH E. BYRNE

PERMANENT ADDRESS
2 Livingston Avenue
Livingston, NJ 07039
201-740-9841

TEMPORARY ADDRESS
Box 1222
Tulane University
New Orleans, LA 70118
504-865-7764

OBJECTIVE   Position in a law firm utilizing research and writing skills.

SKILLS
- Have initiated and completed numerous research projects.
- Can locate and use reference materials to uncover facts, analyze data, and develop written presentations.
- Capable of writing detailed reports and concise, effective synopses.
- Have used printed indexes and database programs for literature searches.
- Can adapt to ever-changing situations and work well under pressure.

EDUCATION   Tulane University, New Orleans, LA
                   Bachelor of Arts, June 1990
                   Major: Anthropology   Minor: Psychology

                   Additional course work in English, history, earth sciences, economics, political science, and public policy.

Honors   Dean's List, Spring 1989 and Fall 1989
and   University Residence Council
Activities   Freshman Adviser
                   Residence Counselor
                   Intramural Athletics

EXPERIENCE
Summers   Herman's World of Sporting Goods, Livingston, NJ

1989   Salesman

1986   Salesman and Cashier

Summers   J and L Hot Dogs, Belmar, NJ

1988   Partner/Operator
1987   Owned and operated hot dog cart in resort community.
                     Net profits--over $5000 for two summers--used for college education.

Summers   Byrne Brothers, Inc., New York, NY

1985   Junior Salesman
                     Participated in all aspects of selling plumbing supplies.

1984   Sales Trainee

INTERESTS   Skiing, tennis, and photography

REFERENCES AND WRITING SAMPLES AVAILABLE UPON REQUEST.

Anthony Canelli:
Many Talents, Many Experiences

Special Features
- A multipurpose functional resume
- Highlights a multitalented, but yet to be focused, job seeker's various skills

The Problem. Anthony Canelli, who majored in diplomacy and world affairs, can do so many things well that he is unsure what he would like to do after graduation. His academic experiences have not been limited to his major field of study. He has minored in mathematics, performing better in his math courses than in those of his major field, and has taken course work in economics, statistics, computer sciences, and Spanish. Anthony's work experiences and extracurricular activities have also contributed to the development of his many talents and capabilities. His problem is his lack of direction.

He has been talking with a career counselor at his college's career planning and placement office in order to decide what he wants to do, but *he wanted to develop a resume he could use in the meantime—one that would be suitable to give to on-campus interviewers and to use in response to posted opportunities.*

The Solution. Anthony decided to stress his skills, and he developed what could be called a traditional functional resume by organizing his accomplishments under skills headings. Reviewing his accomplishments, he identified three basic skill areas that he used to create major headings. These skill areas are presented after Anthony's summary of his educational background.

Anthony felt that his **liberal arts education** gave him the chance to explore many different interests and that it taught him how to view problems in many different ways. Through his course work in mathematics and computer science and several employment experiences, Anthony has learned a great deal about computers and programming applications; he has therefore grouped relevant experiences under a **computer skills heading.** Various jobs have provided Anthony with significant experience in **sales, marketing research, and management,** and since these three activities are often combined in a single job description, Anthony decided to summarize his experience in a separate section on his resume. And finally, because Anthony had demonstrated his responsiveness to **community and social concerns** by serving in political campaigns, community and college events, and the student government, he decided to highlight some of the experiences under yet another skills heading.

Format and Layout. The resume boldly highlights each of Anthony's four headings. Periods before statements serve as bullets to set off specific accomplishments associated with each heading. Shadow type (where the printer has been given the command to strike over a character or series of characters several times) creates a dynamic bolding of the major headings. By using his computer skills to word process (using word processing software, a microcomputer, and a high-quality daisywheel printer), Anthony has allowed himself the flexibility to make easy and quick modifications to format or content. If desired, he can change the order of the major headings to highlight those that are most appropriate for a given position, or he can add an Objective statement.

Summary. The format of this resume is that of a traditional functional resume. Anthony directs attention to major skills categories rather than to specific employers and then documents his accomplishments in each category. Anthony is a person with numerous experiences, many skills, and a great deal to offer an employer. *Until he can focus on specific goals, this resume will serve very nicely.* It communicates to employers that Anthony is a multitalented individual who has many abilities—not just a bright student who knows a lot about diplomacy and world affairs.

Word processed using Courier element. ➡

ANTHONY CANELLI

School Address: Home Address:
534 Dogwood Pl.   12 South Austin Blvd.
Apartment 23A   Champaign, IL 61801
Los Angeles, CA 90042   (217) 333-3857
(213) 259-5682

BROAD LIBERAL ARTS EDUCATION:

OCCIDENTAL COLLEGE, Los Angeles, CA
- Bachelor of Arts, expected June 1990
- Major in Diplomacy and World Affairs--Major GPA 3.2/4.0
- Minor in Mathematics--Minor GPA 3.5/4.0
- Course work in economics, statistics, computer science, and Spanish

AMERICAN UNIVERSITY, Washington, DC
- Through an Occidental College program, worked for Research Council of Washington and completed courses in foreign affairs and government, Fall 1989.

KNOWLEDGEABLE IN COMPUTERS AND PROGRAMMING APPLICATIONS:
- Can program in COBOL and PL/1 languages--GPA in computer science courses 3.45/4.0.
- Familiar with numerous software packages, including Lotus 1-2-3, EXCEL, and dBASE.
- Used variety of hardware, including IBM, DEC, and Apple microcomputers.
- As Research Associate for Research Council of Washington, completed extensive preliminary research for marketing study of home computer sales in Europe, including research of various manufacturers and comparison of their products; used word processor to write and edit final report.
- Developed computer database to present voting records and comparative analyses of voting records of California congressmen and senators on various legislative issues for the League of Women Voters. Summer 1988.
- Provided statistical consulting services and developed software for study of sports injuries for the Occidental College Department of Physical Education. Spring 1988.

EXPERIENCED IN SALES, MARKETING RESEARCH, AND MANAGEMENT:
- Salesperson for College Sporting Goods, Los Angeles, CA, part-time 1988-1990 while attending classes.
- As Assistant Manager for College Sporting Goods, supervised full-time and part-time workers; developed work schedules; opened and closed store; tabulated daily receipts; and received shipments and maintained inventory using a computerized system. Summer 1987.
- Research Council of Washington is a marketing research firm that conducts research on various topics. As Research Associate, undertook thorough literature searches in the Library of Congress; interviewed government officials and trade and industry experts on the telephone to develop detailed reports; and served as a research team leader for a project dealing with home computer sales in Europe.
- Assistant Manager and counterworker for McDonald's, Champaign, IL. Summers and part-time 1985-1987.

RESPONSIVE TO COMMUNITY AND SOCIAL CONCERNS:
- Campaigned for numerous local and national political candidates in California and Illinois.
- Instructor and coach for Southern California Special Olympics. 1988-1990.
- Elected member of Associated Students of Occidental College, student self-governing body, 1989-1990.

Rebecca B. Churchill:
A Music Major's Resume
Hits the High Notes

Special Features
- Targeted, combination functional and chronological resume
- Resume highlights related experiences, tones down education

The Problem. A music history and literature major who did not want to teach, *Rebecca B. Churchill decided to seek a position in human resources management. If possible, she wanted the position to involve training employees.* She had much to offer a potential employer, but she needed a way to stress her qualifications.

The Solution. Rebecca felt that her greatest assets were her fund-raising and administrative experiences, and she developed a resume that emphasized these points. The Qualifications section effectively summarizes her skills and accomplishments and supports her stated Objective by highlighting her experience training personnel and developing training programs. The Related Experience section then provides the nuts-and-bolts details: her job titles, the location of her employers, and when she worked.

Rebecca does not describe her academic experiences in detail, since they are not relevant to her job search goal. In fact, her education credits appear at the very end of the resume.

Format and Layout. Rebecca's resume is designed to draw attention to her greatest strengths: her focused Objective and her relevant qualifications. She begins the resume with a standard block format, in which each sentence begins at the left-hand margin and continues to the right-hand margin. After the first two headings, she uses a two-column format, which helps to emphasize the Professional Objective and Qualifications sections.

Summary. Rebecca is more than a musician; she is a person who has held positions of responsibility in both academic and work settings. By downplaying her education and describing in detail her qualifications in the areas of fund-raising, program supervision, and management, she can be confident that she is presenting herself as a person who has something to offer. Her confidence, and the resume's documentation of her achievements, will serve her well in her job search.

See Rebecca's job search success story on page 99.

REBECCA B. CHURCHILL

Box 23
Hollins College
Roanoke, Virginia 24020
703-369-9645

7765 Wills Circle
Houston, Texas 77024
713-467-9254

PROFESSIONAL OBJECTIVE

Position in human resources management. Special interest in developing and implementing training programs.

QUALIFICATIONS

Developed and directed fund-raising campaign that raised over $150,000 for Ronald McDonald House. Trained 10 team leaders and coordinated efforts of 200 volunteers. Created all training literature and developed a multilevel series of training sessions. Conducted all leader-training sessions and supervised numerous volunteer sessions. Appeared on television to promote efforts. Personally responsible for corporate fund-raising.

Education course work provided knowledge of concepts associated with setting objectives, developing lesson plans and supporting materials, and performing measurable evaluations.

Supervised all arts and crafts activities for YMCA day camp for three summers. Trained counselors and instructed campers in daily projects.

Retail experience with Target Stores involved training new cashiers, assisting with hiring process, and exposure to marketing and customer service.

As temporary office worker, became familiar with personnel procedures of numerous organizations.

RELATED EXPERIENCE

Ronald McDonald House
Roanoke, Virginia
Chairperson, Fund-raising Committee

Developed campaign to raise funds to purchase and renovate house for use by families with children who are receiving treatment for severe illnesses. Part-time, 1987–1989

Norrell Services, Inc.
Houston, Texas
Temporary Office Worker

Performed clerical and reception duties for various organizations. Summer 1988

Target Stores, Inc.
Houston, Texas
Pharmacy Clerk
Assistant Head Cashier and Cashier

As Pharmacy Clerk, maintained prescription files, assisted customers, and tabulated receipts. Winter 1988

As Assistant Head Cashier, developed work schedules for all cashiers, took register totals, and balanced all cash drawers. Part-time 1984–1986

Summer of Fun Day Camp
Houston, Texas
Arts and Crafts Director

Planned and taught all arts and crafts activities, budgeted for and purchased all materials, and trained counselors. Summers 1985–1987

EDUCATION

Hollins College, Roanoke, Virginia
Bachelor of Arts, December 1989
Major: Music History and Literature
Activities: Mu Phi Epsilon Music Fraternity and
   Student Judiciary Committee

Overall Grade Point Average: 3.2/4.0
Major Grade Point Average: 3.3/4.0

Christopher Crockett:
Looking For a Trial Career or
"Prelaw Preparation"

Special Features
- Boldly highlights skills before anything else
- Multipurpose resume combining functional and chronological approaches

---

The Problem. Christopher Crockett is majoring in history and Spanish, and he thinks that he will someday attend law school, it being something of a family tradition. He is still not sure, however, that attending law school would be a conscious choice and not just an unconscious following of others' expectations. "Law school would be the easy way to go, but I would like to try something else first to give myself time to decide whether I really want to be a lawyer." *Because he lacked a clear career goal, Chris created a resume that highlights the skills he developed throughout his numerous extracurricular and work experiences.*

The Solution. Chris's greatest assets are stressed at the very beginning of his resume. Under the headings Program Design and Implementation and Research and Report Writing, he describes in active and functional terms the experiences he has had that have developed these capabilities. Under Experience, Chris gives further details about these experiences: names of organizations and people he worked with, dates, locations, and so on. A potential employer who reads the entire resume will conclude that Christopher Crockett is a person who has done a great deal in the past and will continue to do a great deal in the future.

Without definite focus, but aware of at least three possible job search directions, including international banking, translation or other work for international organizations, and a staff position in Washington, D.C., Chris created a resume that would be appropriate for any of these (and for many other possibilities). Chris is aware that his resume cannot be all things to all potential employers and that he will have to stress different aspects of his past in cover letters and during interviews, depending on the requirements of the job. For positions in banking, for example, he will emphasize his research and writing skills and his ability to promote ideas. For positions that might require him to travel or deal with international organizations, he will draw attention to his foreign travel experiences and fluency in Spanish. For posts in Washington, Chris will stress his previous experiences as a congressional intern, as well as his committee work and experiences as a program planner.

Format and Layout. The layout of Chris's resume is unique in that the listing of skills appears at the beginning without a major introductory heading such as Skills or Summary of Skills. This is because Chris wanted to draw the attention of individual employers to specific skills, not to a total summary of his skills. As discussed, he will "target" his cover letters and interview presentations, focusing on the skills he feels would be important to a given employer. Boldface type and the use of several different type sizes and styles enable Chris to highlight words and phrases that are of most importance.

Summary. Christopher Crockett is a double-major liberal arts graduate with a history of success. Given the opportunity, he will translate past accomplishments into future successes. This resume will help him express his past in a skills language that potential employers will understand and that should translate into job search success.

Typeset in Palatino. ➡

CHRISTOPHER CROCKETT

326 Main Street, 3E
Hanover, NH 03755
(603) 643-2369

PROGRAM DESIGN AND IMPLEMENTATION

As **member of committee** that organized and presented a three-day conference called "Nuclear Arms: Challenge and Choices," assisted in developing program focus, invited nationally known speakers, arranged transportation and accommodations for speakers, reserved facilities for seminars and speakers, and coordinated efforts of over 100 student and staff volunteers.

As **Apprentice Teacher,** developed and implemented daily lesson plans designed to fit into a total framework of course objectives.

As **Alumni Language Program Assistant,** taught, developed, and implemented lesson plans and assisted in organizing ten-day program involving participants of all ages, backgrounds, and language proficiencies. Coordinated registration and housing, organized programs, and acted as a liaison between program organizers and participants.

While serving in **numerous elected positions,** planned programs, delegated responsibilities, and oversaw work of peers to ensure program completion.

RESEARCH AND REPORT WRITING

As **Congressional Intern,** researched and analyzed policy issues and prospective legislation and wrote policy analyses and synopses. Corresponded with constituents concerning various local and national issues. Utilized Library of Congress for research.

As **Paralegal,** researched issues dealing with pending cases, searched titles, and wrote preliminary briefs.

As **Senior and Junior Class President,** wrote numerous reports to administration presenting student viewpoint on college issues.

EDUCATION

DARTMOUTH COLLEGE, Hanover, NH. Class of 1990.
Double major in history and Spanish, concentration in history of Latin America and international affairs. Fluent in Spanish.

UNIVERSIDAD DE GRANADA, Granada, Spain
Studied history, literature, and art as a part of Dartmouth's Language Study Abroad Program. Spring 1988.

SAN ANTONIO HIGH SCHOOL, San Antonio, TX. Class of 1986.
Delivered valedictory address. Member of National Honor Society. President of Junior Class. President of Spanish Club.

EXPERIENCE

DARTMOUTH COLLEGE SPANISH DEPARTMENT, Hanover, NH. Winter 1989–Spring 1990.
Apprentice Teacher: Taught Spanish using Rassias method utilizing intensive language drills. Devised and presented daily drill sessions to classes of 10 to 15 students. Assisted in preparation of examinations and reviewed homework.

DARTMOUTH COLLEGE SENIOR SYMPOSIUM COMMITTEE, Hanover, NH. Winter 1989–Spring 1990.
Executive Committee Member: Involved in organization and coordination of three-day symposium that brought several nationally known speakers to campus to discuss issues related to nuclear arms development. Symposium received network news coverage.

DARTMOUTH COLLEGE ALUMNI LANGUAGE PROGRAM, Hanover, NH. Summer 1989.
Student Assistant: Working under Professor John Rassias, taught Spanish to participants of all ages. Developed and presented lessons and drill sessions. Organized logistics of ten-day program, including housing, registration, and activities. Interacted with people of various backgrounds and taught all levels of language skills.

CROCKETT AND TAGLE, ATTORNEYS-AT-LAW, San Antonio, TX. Summers 1988 and 1987.
Paralegal: Researched issues for pending cases, searched titles, and wrote preliminary briefs. Gained working knowledge of basic legal tenets.

HONORABLE HENRY B. GONZALEZ, Washington, DC. Fall 1987.
Congressional Intern: Researched and analyzed policy issues including economic development, U.S.-Mexican relations, tax law changes, and the federal budget. Drafted responses to constituents' questions and corresponded with constituents. Served as assistant to congressman's press aide.

DARTMOUTH ACTIVITIES

Elected Senior and Junior Class President.

Member, Alpha Theta Fraternity.

Member, Paleopitus, a leadership organization that presents student viewpoints on various issues to the administration.

Member, Honorary Degree Committee.

Member, Green Key, junior honorary society that provides a wide range of services to the college community.

REFERENCES AVAILABLE UPON REQUEST.

Parker C. Davidson:
The Astronomy Major Who Wants to Be
a Star—But Where?

Special Feature
• Multipurpose chronological resume that can be used in applying for jobs and filling out graduate school applications

The Problem. Like many liberal arts students, Parker C. Davidson, an astronomy major, faces a difficult decision upon graduation. He is not sure whether to seek entry-level employment or enter law school or an M.B.A. program. He seems to be a natural at sales and marketing, but he has doubts about whether, with a major in astronomy, he has adequate preparation to advance in business. He is a very ambitious person who wishes to excel at whatever he does.

In addition to considering entry-level positions in marketing and sales, as well as law-related areas, Parker wants to explore the possibility of teaching and coaching in a private secondary school for a few years prior to entering graduate school. Talented in academics, sports, and singing, he wants what he calls "a last opportunity to be in an environment where I can do all three and get paid for it."

The Solution. Parker developed a traditional chronological resume that will enable him to present himself as a multitalented, success-oriented person. Because of its simplicity, it allows Parker to direct attention to specific academic, extracurricular, or job-related items, according to his purposes. Parker's high school scholastic and athletic achievements are worth mentioning, even though they are normally omitted from a resume. The diversity of his academic and extracurricular activities will be very attractive to private schools. He can teach science, computer science, foreign languages, and economics, as well as coach football or track and direct vocal groups.

Parker can use his resume not only to apply for jobs but also to apply to graduate and professional schools. It will make completing applications to law schools and graduate business schools easier, for all of the background information requested on such forms appears on the resume and will be easy for him to transcribe.

Format and Layout. Although Parker uses a traditional chronological approach, his resume does not look boring. He uses bullets (typed periods) to highlight extracurricular and employment accomplishments. A timeline down the margin indicates when he was involved in each of his numerous activities. Parker also uses capitalization and italics to emphasize important information.

Summary. Parker Davidson the astronomy major wants to be a star wherever he goes after graduation. The confusion he faces now will not lessen his chances of shining within any of the numerous settings he is considering. He has a resume that is effective, and he will act assertively in communicating with people in each of these settings.

PARKER C. DAVIDSON

School Address
3529 Montgomery Avenue
Haverford, PA 19041
(215) 648-8786

Home Address
29 Lake Forest Lane
Lake Forest, IL 62541
(708) 767-8982

EDUCATION

1986–1990   HAVERFORD COLLEGE, Haverford, PA
B.A. in Astronomy, June 1990. Overall GPA: 3.2/4.0. Academic Honors junior year, anticipated for senior year. Course work in macroeconomics, microeconomics, international affairs, comparative political systems. Knowledge of BASIC and related computer languages. Fluent in German. Proficient in French.

- Varsity Football 1987–1989—Letterman 1988 and 1989.
- Haverford A Cappella Singers 1986–1990—Musical Director 1989–1990: arranged music for performances, conducted rehearsals, coordinated record album production efforts.
- Haverford Chamber Singers 1987.
- Thanksgiving Food Drive and other community service projects.

1983–1986   LAKE FOREST HIGH SCHOOL, Lake Forest, IL
Graduated 16th out of class of 435, June 1986. National Honor Society. Cum Laude Society. National Merit Commendation. Illinois State Scholar.

- Varsity Football 1983–1985—Letterman 1983, 1984, and 1985.
- Varsity Track 1984–1986—Letterman 1985 and 1986.
- Forester Singers and Madrigal and Swing vocal groups.
- Eagle Scout.

EMPLOYMENT

1989–1990   NATIONAL DIRECTORY OF SUMMER INTERNSHIPS, Haverford, PA
Marketing Director

- Coordinated marketing efforts for student-published directory.
- Developed mailing list and brochures.
- Received orders and shipped directories.
- Maintained financial records.
- Efforts resulted in largest-ever sales of directory—over 4,000 copies—and largest net profit—over $7500.

1988
Summer   AMERICAN HOSPITAL SUPPLY CORPORATION, McGaw Park, IL
Market Research Intern, American Critical Care Division

- Coordinated distribution and data analysis for New Products Questionnaire.
- Designed and completed Sales Tracking Studies and Market Overview Studies.
- Assisted salespersons in direct-sales efforts.

1987 and
1986
Summers   SMITH'S MEN'S STORE, Lake Forest, IL
Salesperson

- Assisted customers with purchases.
- Tabulated sales receipts.
- Displayed merchandise and maintained stock.
- Opened and closed store.
- Trained new personnel.

INTERESTS

Politics, tennis, golf, literature, theater, and music.

James Dawson:
A Journalist Shows His
Skills and His Works

Special Features
- Combination resume and portfolio
- Creative graphic presentation and format
- Targeted resume including Objective statement and Qualifications section

The Problem. James Dawson's greatest assets are his job search focus and job-related experience. *This philosophy major's resume is targeted to project a sense of direction and determination; it contains an Objective, a Qualifications section, and a Related Experience section to reinforce the fact that James has had exposure to communications industry settings and tasks and that he seeks an opportunity to use his talents in this field.* James's diverse job-related experiences are first cited in the Qualifications section and then documented in the list of employers and job titles appearing under Related Experience.

The Solution. Over the course of the years, while working at a number of interesting jobs in communications, James had been able to collect a number of impressive samples that could be used to demonstrate the quality of his work to potential employers. In trying to think of creative ways to present these samples, James came up with a novel idea. He made his resume into a portfolio. (Creativity is of course one of James's strengths, and his original approach to resume writing demonstrates this very well.)

Format and Layout. James's resume was printed on 11-x-17-inch paper, folded like a book. The resume itself appears on the outside cover and his samples appear on the inside right-hand page under the heading "Samples of Work by James Dawson" (see illustration at right). Under this heading James can attach copies of his best works. He always included photos and often sent along a few writing samples as well. He based his selection of samples on the type of organization he was contacting and always included brief abstracts summarizing the assignments, purposes, and logistics associated with each sample. Thus he attached more newspaper stories when contacting newspapers and more magazine stories when contacting magazines. The finished product looks very professional and projects creativity and knowledge of layout and design.

Special Uses. James used the resume when applying for admission to a summer publishing course. After completing the program the summer after graduation, James entered this experience under the Education heading.

Summary. By means of this special resume James is able to tell employers about his qualifications and actually show them samples of work. James's resume truly "shows and tells" employers that he has the skills to succeed.

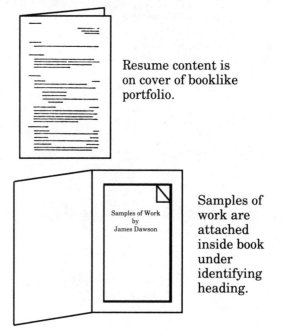

Resume content is on cover of booklike portfolio.

Samples of Work
by
James Dawson

Samples of work are attached inside book under identifying heading.

JAMES DAWSON

Box 835 Trinity College
Hartford, CT 06106
(203) 527-8643

OBJECTIVE

A position requiring skills in writing, editing, and photography.

QUALIFICATIONS

Experience in magazine, newspaper, and book publishing . . . edited for style and content . . . researched for accuracy . . . assigned, supplemented, and revised stories . . . coordinated photographs and artwork . . . possess thorough command of grammar . . . knowledge of layout and design.

EDUCATION

TRINITY COLLEGE   Hartford, CT
Bachelor of Arts degree, with major in Philosophy.
June 1990. Studied at the Institute for European Studies, London, England.

  Varsity Squash (1986–1990)
  Black Students Association (1986–1990)
  Trinity Tripod: reporter and photographer for weekly campus newspaper (1987–1990)

STANFORD PUBLISHING COURSE   Stanford, CA
Completed course requirements, summer 1990. Participated in seminars presented by representatives of national publishing houses and magazines on editorial, design, and marketing aspects of publishing. As final project, devised editorial content, cover and interior design, and direct-mail package for hypothetical magazine.

RELATED EXPERIENCE

WEST HARTFORD NEWS   West Hartford, CT
Reporter. Covered town news and features for weekly newspaper. (Part-time, 1988–1990)

D MAGAZINE   Dallas, TX
Intern. Edited copy, wrote articles, conducted telephone interviews and polls, and organized photograph files. (Summer 1989)

TEXAS HOMES MAGAZINE   Dallas, TX
Intern. Edited copy, participated in house shoots, wrote letters to writers concerning unsolicited manuscripts and story ideas, corresponded with writers concerning assignments, and searched for article illustrations. (Summer 1989)

DC PUBLIC RELATIONS   Dallas, TX
Account Assistant. Assisted in preparation of campaign proposals, researched client background information, created slogans, took photographs, and solicited new accounts. (Summer 1988)

NEW LONDON PRESS   Dallas, TX
Editorial Assistant. Proofread and pasted up copy, wrote biographies of authors for publicity materials, and researched bibliographies. (Summer 1987)

Jennifer Drew:
From Elementary to Higher Education—
Bridging the Gap

Special Features
- Targeted functional resume used to make the transition from one field to another
- Transferable Skills and Capabilities section highlights the skills from the field of elementary education that are applicable to higher education

The Problem. Jennifer Drew has an undergraduate degree in elementary education and a graduate degree in bilingual education. After teaching in an elementary school bilingual education program for over four years, she now wants "out." She wants to leave the setting she is in, but she does not want to leave the field of education. She feels she would rather apply the skills she has to positions in higher education. *As a result of consulting with some of her undergraduate college's alumni and participating in a number of informational interviews, Jennifer became very interested in development and admissions work.* Since she now had new career goals in mind, Jennifer wanted to be careful not to project the image of an elementary school teacher who was tired of "minding the kids." She wanted to present herself as a person who has direction and who has talents that are applicable to her new goals. Jennifer therefore developed a functional resume that stressed skills, rather than job titles, degrees, or dates.

The Solution. Jennifer stresses direction and a skills perspective by using linked Career Goal and Transferable Skills and Capabilities sections. She highlights her communications, organization and program planning, and language capabilities. A potential employer reading Jennifer's resume will perceive her as a person who has real, transferable qualifications and not just as a teacher who wants to change careers. Within the discussions of skills, Jennifer presents evidence of the abilities she gained from experiences outside the area of elementary education. Jennifer has done much more than just teach young people; she has organized events, planned programs, raised funds, and been involved in numerous activities that

required various skills and capabilities. By writing a targeted cover letter, Jennifer can describe in more detail the skills and experiences that would be applicable to a particular employer. She can elaborate upon her fund-raising activities, persuasive skills, and research capabilities when applying for development jobs and highlight her communications, sales, and evaluation skills when applying for admissions positions. By identifying examples of how her skills can be used in her desired setting, Jennifer is highlighting the capabilities she possesses to succeed on the job. She is connecting her past experiences to qualifications associated with her anticipated future.

Format and Layout. Jennifer developed a resume that presents her as a person who is capable of functioning well within higher education. By presenting skills at the beginning of the resume—following a statement of career goal—and her teaching positions and academic training in elementary education at the end, Jennifer succeeds in doing what all career changers must do—she builds a "skills bridge" from her past to the future. Jennifer's resume tells potential employers that what she has done can be applied to what she will do in future jobs.

Summary. Jennifer is not just a collection of job titles and academic degrees. She is a person who is capable of performing the tasks associated with her new job search targets, and her resume shows a potential employer that this is the case. It bridges the gap between elementary education and student services positions in higher education.

JENNIFER DREW

229 Brokenbend Road
Los Angeles, CA 90017
213-746-3953

CAREER GOAL

To use the following skills and capabilities within higher education.
Special interest in development and admissions positions.

TRANSFERABLE SKILLS AND CAPABILITIES

Knowledge of Diverse Academic Settings

Attended private and public colleges and universities and worked within varied school systems. Worked in alumni affairs capacities, as Hiram College Class of 1985 Vice President, setting goals, motivating volunteers, and presenting information.
- Capable of identifying distinct characteristics of institutions, working within existing structures, and presenting appropriate information to targeted audiences.
- Capable of establishing relationships with targeted school districts and potential donors.

Research and Analysis

Have practical and theoretical background, which required setting goals and performance criteria, developing programs to meet goals, and developing measurement techniques to evaluate individual and group performance. Used standardized aptitude and achievement tests to assess for tracking purposes.
- Capable of setting selection criteria, creating evaluation measures, and evaluating applicants.
- Capable of researching backgrounds and using knowledge to develop effective solicitation strategies.

Communications and Presentations

Chaired fund-raising events for school and church groups. Communicated weekly with parents regarding student progress and with administrators regarding classroom activities and budget requests. Counseled students on personal and academic issues. Trained and supervised student teachers. Worked with emergency room patients and staff as volunteer translator.
- Capable of working with, training, and motivating volunteer groups.
- Capable of developing persuasive presentations and communicating with individuals with multicultural backgrounds in a variety of settings. Fluent in Spanish; familiar with French.

Organization and Program Planning

Developed individual and group activities. Motivated and supervised student participation. Created individualized programs to help students attain specific objectives. Assisted in establishing a local/national grant-funded School Improvement Plan that increased efficiency of programs and improved community relations. Completed detailed federal, state, and local documentation accurately and on time.
- Capable of organizing programs and presentations, taking actions to support attendance, and motivating the efforts of others.
- Capable of identifying grants, writing proposals, and completing reports.

EDUCATION

M.Ed. University of California, Los Angeles, Los Angeles, CA.
       Bilingual Education, December 1988. Course work in Education Administration.

B.A.   Hiram College, Hiram, OH.
       Elementary Education, June 1985.

EMPLOYMENT HISTORY

Los Angeles Unified School District, Los Angeles, CA.
    Bilingual Teacher, 1985–present.
Cleveland Independent School District, Cleveland, OH.
    Student Teacher, 1984–1985.
Davidson's Department Store, Cleveland, OH.
    Salesperson, part-time and summers 1981–1984.

ACTIVITIES AND ASSOCIATIONS

Hiram College Alumni Association, Class of 1985 Vice President.
UCLA Medical Center, Volunteer.
American Association of Bilingual Educators.
American Teachers Association.

Kathy Fish:
Presenting Career-Transferable Skills

Special Features
- Multipurpose resume suitable for more than one job search interest
- Career-Transferable Skills section

The Problem. Kathy Fish, who majored in government, suffered from the so-called "plight of the liberal arts graduate." She believed that her education had given her nothing to present to a potential employer and that she had no marketable skills. A visit to her college's career planning and placement office "cured" Kathy or perhaps "rediagnosed" her ailment. Kathy suffered from lack of awareness and lack of confidence—she was unaware of all of the skills she possessed and had no confidence in her ability to present herself to a potential employer as a person worth hiring. Although she had not defined specific goals, Kathy did have a resume that she was proud of and some idea of where she was looking.

The Solution. Self-assessment and the completion of the Skills Inventory and Skills Flowchart made Kathy aware of the many qualities she had to offer an employer. Research into career options gave her some ideas about which areas to focus on. *As of the time she wrote her resume, the fields she had tentatively settled on included banking operations, state government, and college student personnel.* Kathy felt that banking operations would be an excellent setting in which to use almost all of her skills and her course work in economics, accounting, and computer programming. Her interest in state government stems from her experiences with a political campaign, and her interest in college student personnel work stems from her experience in the financial aid office of her college. The resume Kathy developed can be used effectively in each of these areas.

Kathy's assessment of her skills enabled her to create the section that appears at the bottom of her resume, appropriately titled "Career-Transferable Skills." Under each type of skill, she outlines the experience she has had that most directly involved use of the skill. In her communications with potential employers, in cover letters and during interviews, Kathy will draw upon this portion of her resume to support her candidacy for employment.

If Kathy becomes more interested in one of the above three areas, she can target her resume by adding a statement of Objective and by reworking the skills section and moving it to appear immediately after the Objective. If she decides on banking operations, for example, she can change the heading to "Banking Skills," use the same skills headings, and add to the descriptions analyses of how they would enhance her performance as a person working within bank operations. For now, she is pleased with the resume as it is.

Format and Layout. Kathy's resume is fairly conservative in appearance, which is appropriate for the fields she is considering. She used capitalization to create prominent headings and italics to make some of the most important phrases stand out. One of the best features of this resume is the Career-Transferable Skills section. Kathy chose to save the best for last, summarizing her qualifications and the skills she acquired from all of the experiences cited under the Education and Experience headings as well as from some experiences not cited.

Summary. This resume presents Kathy's assets very well. For Kathy the cure for the plight of the liberal arts student was a dose of awareness and self-confidence brought about by a careful and thoughtful assessment of her skills and the resulting realization that she too could produce a very professional looking resume for herself.

See Kathy's job search success story on page 101.

KATHY FISH

HOME ADDRESS
198 Vine Street
Damariscotta, Maine 04543
207-563-1972

SCHOOL ADDRESS
352B Main Street
Brunswick, Maine 04011
207-724-3356

EDUCATION

BOWDOIN COLLEGE   Brunswick, ME
Bachelor of Arts, May 1990.
Honors major in Government (GPA 3.4/4.0), with emphasis on analysis and comparisons of political systems.
Courses included international organizations, macroeconomics, microeconomics, international economics, accounting, and computer programming (C and FORTRAN).
Foreign study in Paris, France. Fluent in French. College exchange with Dartmouth College, fall 1988.
Class of 1990 Executive Committee. Inter-Dormitory Committee. Dormitory Chairperson 1987. Women's Track. Women's Rugby. Glee Club. Intramural Sports.

LINCOLN ACADEMY   Newcastle, ME
Graduated *Valedictorian,* June 1986. Selected for AFS International Student Exchange to Salvador, Brazil, 1985. National Honor Society. Senior Class President. Maine Scholar's Day Delegate.

EXPERIENCE

BOWDOIN COLLEGE OFFICE OF FINANCIAL AID   Brunswick, ME
Student Assistant. Assist students in completing financial aid forms. Review applications, calculating need analyses and submitting forms to financial aid officers for final decisions. Complete Work-Study and other federal paperwork. Maintain student files. (September 1989–present)

BOWDOIN COLLEGE GOVERNMENT DEPARTMENT   Brunswick, ME
Research Assistant. Aided professor with research project. Results presented at an international symposium in Rio de Janeiro, Brazil. (March–June 1988)

THE CHEECHAKO RESTAURANT   Damariscotta, ME
Waitress. Supervised dining room personnel. Analyzed and accounted for dining room receipts. (Summers 1987, 1986, and 1985)

Assumed full responsibility for meeting costs of college education.

CAREER-TRANSFERABLE SKILLS

RESEARCH AND ANALYTICAL SKILLS
Selected as research assistant by professor in Government Department. Gathered and analyzed data regarding the effect of economic factors in the formation of political systems in Spain and Portugal. Developed and conducted independent research study dealing with politicization of children; results were used in research paper.

ORGANIZATIONAL SKILLS
Assisted with design and coordination of 300-person telephone survey concerning campaign issues involved in Maine Senate race. Recruited and trained surveyors. Wrote reports concerning results. Maintained financial aid files for over 750 students.

INTERPERSONAL SKILLS
Experienced in training and managing fellow workers, counseling peers, and representing peers in elected positions. Lived with two non-English-speaking families as part of foreign-study experiences. Advised and counseled students on financial aid issues. Motivated volunteer workers to contribute time and money to political campaign.

Elaine S. Fletcher:
Back to Work for Someone
Who Never Stopped

Special Features
- Resume for reentry into the job market highlights many accomplishments
- Qualifications section summarizes greatest strengths

The Problem. Elaine S. Fletcher wants to reenter the working world after ten years spent caring for her family, and she needs to let potential employers in on all the things she accomplished while she wasn't "working." Although she wasn't paid for her labors, Elaine was a very active member of her community. She held positions of responsibility on various committees, positions that allowed her to develop and utilize skills that are applicable to conventional work settings. Elaine had also continued to pursue her educational interests. In order to show employers that she hadn't only been keeping house and raising a family, Elaine developed a resume that presents her as someone who never stopped learning and participating.

The Solution. Elaine is what one would call a "doer"; she is always actively involved in something. After graduation from college, Elaine started working for an insurance company. With the birth of her first child Elaine stopped working for the insurance company, but she didn't stop doing. She began taking adult-education classes at a local high school and, not one to just take classes, she became very actively involved in the administration of the adult-education program. Because of her work experiences with the insurance company and her summer job with a savings and loan, and because she had taken accounting, Elaine was eventually elected an Executive Board Member. In that capacity, she became involved in the board of education's Administrative Review Committee. As if that weren't enough, Elaine was also an active member of her church's College and Service Outreach Program (a program she herself developed several years ago) and a leader of a Brownie Girl Scout troop.

It should be clear by now that Elaine never really stopped working after she left the insurance

company. She continued to grow as a person—and as a potential employee—developing and using skills that should be of interest to many employers. Although Elaine is unsure of exactly what type of job she wants, she is sure that she is ready to return to the so-called working world. The Career Decision Making course Elaine took at a local community college got her started on the career decision-making process and taught her some very useful research and job search techniques. *Elaine will use the resume she developed as an exercise for that class in order to communicate with potential employers.*

Format and Layout. Elaine had her resume typeset in order to project a very businesslike image and to show employers that she is serious about finding a job. Her resume starts with a Qualifications section that presents a summary of all the skills Elaine developed over the course of the years. Elaine decided to highlight her educational background, not because she wanted to put her Home Economics degree to use, but because she was proud of the fact that she has never stopped learning. She listed several of the community college and adult-education courses she had taken. Under Community Leadership Elaine details the various positions she held that involved hours and hours of work and required many different skills.

Summary. Elaine did not stop learning or working after she left her job with the insurance company almost ten years ago. She will use this resume to find another job in which she can apply all that she has learned over the years. She will no doubt continue to work as hard in a paid position as she has in her volunteer capacities.

ELAINE S. FLETCHER

223 Burgundy Drive
Flint, Michigan 48506
(313) 762-9753

QUALIFICATIONS

Experienced bookkeeper and organizer. Capable of maintaining Accounts Receivable and Accounts Payable. Capable of supervising others and motivating others to maintain optimum performance levels. Can develop and implement projects, paying attention to detail and meeting deadlines. Have worked on committees and in group settings. Have established performance standards and evaluated employees' performance.

EDUCATION

MICHIGAN STATE UNIVERSITY, East Lansing, Michigan
Bachelor of Arts in Home Economics, June 1978

LANSING COMMUNITY COLLEGE, Lansing, Michigan (1974–1976)

Additional Educational Experiences:

MOTT COMMUNITY COLLEGE, Flint, Michigan
"Introduction to Home Computers," Spring 1988
"Career Decision Making," Fall 1987
"Introduction to Accounting," Fall 1978

FLINT HIGH SCHOOL ADULT EDUCATION PROGRAM, Flint, Michigan
"Management Skills," Winter 1985
"Group Dynamics," Winter 1984
"Personal Financial Management," Winter 1983
"European Art," Winter 1982
"Interior Decorating," Winter 1981

EMPLOYMENT BACKGROUND

MINNESOTA MUTUAL LIFE INSURANCE CO., Flint, Michigan (1978–1980)
As Group Claims Coordinator, coordinated transactions and maintained records of all health-care and hospitalization claims. Recorded additions, deletions, conversions, payments, and reconciliations, and acted upon claim-eligibility requests. Handled mail and telephone inquiries and corresponded directly with subscribers.

LANSING SAVINGS AND LOAN, Lansing, Michigan (summers and part-time 1975–1978)
As Teller, handled all banking transactions, including checking, savings, loan and mortgage payments, and savings bonds.

COMMUNITY LEADERSHIP

FLINT HIGH SCHOOL ADULT EDUCATION PROGRAM, Flint, Michigan (1982–present)
As Treasurer, maintain all financial records and administer budget of over $50,000 each year. (1983–present)
As Executive Board Member, develop goals and policies for adult education program, interview and hire instructors, and interact with board of education members concerning budget and policy matters. (1982–present)

FLINT BOARD OF EDUCATION ADMINISTRATIVE REVIEW COMMITTEE, Flint, Michigan (1988–present)
As Committee Member, interview teachers and administrators concerning academic and administrative policies, evaluate policies and personnel, and make recommendations to the board of education. The purpose of the committee is to identify inefficiency, eliminate duplicated efforts, and cut $1,500,000 from the budget.

MAPLE AVENUE METHODIST CHURCH, Flint, Michigan (1980–present)
Wrote proposal that resulted in College and Service Outreach Program for college students and persons in the armed services who are church members. Solicited church sponsor families to communicate with program members while they were away at school or on duty. Maintain complete records of all program members. Administered program 1980–1982. Remain active in program as sponsor and as member of coordinating committee.

GIRL SCOUTS OF AMERICA—FLINT COUNCIL, Flint, Michigan (1986–present)
As Girl Scout Leader, responsible for troop of approximately 15 girls. Plan and coordinate activities and maintain troop financial records.

REFERENCES

Available upon request.

Cathy Lynne Giles:
Banking Past, Present, and Future

Special Features
- Targeted resume with very focused statement of career goal
- Banking Qualifications section reviews credentials specific to job search goal
- A Sales Experience heading highlights corollary experience

Cathy Lynne Giles is a very focused individual. *She knows that she wants to be a loan officer in a commercial bank.* Whether she enters the field through a formalized lending training program or through an entry-level position that will at least provide some exposure to lending matters very little to her. Fortunately, Cathy has had a significant amount of experience in banking. Several of her summer and part-time jobs in banks have already taught her a lot about the nature of the work and helped her decide on her career goal.

Cathy targets her resume by using Career Goal, Banking Qualifications, Banking Experience, and Sales Experience headings. Her goal is stated at the very beginning of the resume, and the Qualifications section, appearing immediately after the goal statement, summarizes all of the qualities that would make Cathy a good candidate. Cathy does not include the names of organizations she has worked for in the Qualifications section, but she does make clear references to the types of experiences she has had. Names, dates, and details about her jobs are presented in the following sections of Cathy's resume. To help orient potential employers and to emphasize the fact that she has had experience both in banking and in retail and direct sales, Cathy grouped her listings of former jobs under two separate headings.

Format and Layout. This combined functional and chronological format is truly the best for someone like Cathy who has both a clear job search target and related experiences. It will be obvious to anyone who reads the resume that Cathy is qualified for the position she seeks.

Even though she majored in economics, Cathy felt that her work experiences would do more to help her get a job than would her education, so she listed her academic credentials after her work history. Note that Cathy included the names, addresses, and phone numbers of former employers who agreed to provide references; printing this information on the resume can help save time during the application process, but it is not an approach that every job seeker should use. By noting two banking-related references, Cathy continues to project a strong track record within her field of interest. Of course, she could have created a separate reference sheet to attach to her resume when desired.

Summary. Cathy's resume speaks for itself. It is well written and well presented, and Cathy's goals and qualifications come across loudly and clearly. Cathy has worked in banks while in college; the resume she has developed will ensure that she will be able to do so after graduation.

See Cathy's job search success story on page 102.

CATHY LYNNE GILES
232 Aldridge Avenue
Winter Park, Florida 32789
(407) 645-8922

CAREER GOAL
Commercial bank loan officer.

BANKING QUALIFICATIONS
- Experience in banking and researching banking-related legislation. Commitment to a career in banking.
- Course work in economics, including money and banking, accounting, finance, computer science, and research techniques.
- Retail and direct-sales experience.
- Possess the skills required to research loan applicants and assess the risk associated with loans. Can sell successfully and maintain good relationships with customers.

BANKING EXPERIENCE

1989–1990   WINTER PARK BANK AND TRUST COMPANY, Winter Park, Florida.
Teller (15 hours/week)
Performed all teller transactions, including checking, savings, and certificates of deposit. Answered inquiries concerning bank services. Opened new accounts.

Summers
1988 and
1989   NORTHPARK NATIONAL BANK, Dallas, Texas.
Trust Department Intern (full-time)
Developed efficient procedure for processing stock and bond certificates of various banks to be exchanged for holding-company stock. Prepared weekly progress reports for large trust funds and created an indexing and filing system for quick retrieval of information in the forms of summaries and original reports.

Winter
1988   STATE SENATOR MARYANN MATHERS, Tallahassee, Florida.
Administrative Assistant (full-time)
Briefed Senator on legislation. Researched and drafted bills. Attended committee meetings. Corresponded with constituents. Completed primary research on bill regarding interstate banking.

SALES EXPERIENCE

Summer
1987   SANGER-HARRIS, Dallas, Texas.
Sportswear Salesperson (full-time)
Assisted customers with selections. Maintained inventory records and tabulated department sales on daily, weekly, and monthly bases.

1984–1987   MARY KAY COSMETICS, Dallas, Texas.
Sales Associate/Consultant (part-time and summers)
Assessed individual customers' needs and sold cosmetics and beauty supplies. Made numerous presentations to large gatherings. Always achieved sales goals. Was youngest person to be promoted to Consultant level.

EDUCATION

1986–1990   ROLLINS COLLEGE, Winter Park, Florida.
Bachelor of Arts, anticipated June 1990.
Major: Economics
Banking-related course work: Macroeconomics, Microeconomics, Introduction to Accounting, Money and Banking, International Finance, Fundamentals of Computer Science (FORTRAN and COBOL), Analyses of Political Systems, and Research Methodologies.

REFERENCES

Mr. Ralph Stanky
Vice President
Manager, Trust Department
Northpark National Bank
P.O. Box 2319
Dallas, Texas 75294
(214) 783-7777

Ms. Linda Motek
Vice President, Operations
Winter Park Bank and Trust Company
P.O. Box 222
Winter Park, Florida 32788
(407) 643-9988

State Senator Maryann Mathers
State Capitol, 3-784
Tallahassee, Florida 32304
(904) 336-1115

Gloria E. Glenn:
From Sociology to Computer Sales

Special Features
- Skills and Qualifications section used to focus attention on goal-related skills and experiences
- Resume shows a sociology major can project herself as the ideal candidate for a computer-sales job
- Targeted resume can be broadened for other objectives

The Problem. Gloria E. Glenn's major and the degree she will receive bear little direct application to her job search goal. But Gloria does possess the background and motivation to succeed in a sales-oriented environment. She has worked in retail sales throughout high school and college and has promoted herself and her ideas while participating in numerous extracurricular activities.

The Solution. Developing a Professional Objective statement to target her resume was easy for Gloria. *A review of her past accomplishments and of her present interests led her to the conclusion that a position in computer hardware or software sales would be ideal.* Having reached this conclusion, Gloria then spent a great deal of time carefully developing the Skills and Qualifications section; this is the "hook" of her resume, the part that will catch the attention of potential employers. It serves as a preface of sorts and is intended to motivate a potential employer to keep reading. A well-thought-out Skills and Qualifications section can also influence the decision-making process in a positive way.

Some of the courses and experiences Gloria had at the University of Oklahoma and Lamar University are, of course, directly applicable to her job search goal, but Gloria chose to put Educational Background at the end of her resume. She highlights factors she judges more important at the beginning, citing course work in calculus, statistics, computer science, and research techniques in the Skills and Qualifications section rather than in Educational Background.

Special Uses. If Gloria wished to develop a second resume to seek entry-level positions outside the area of technical sales, all she would have to do is eliminate or change the Objective statement and

replace or move, if she wanted to highlight other skill areas, the "technical knowledge" section in her listing of Skills and Qualifications. In this way she could create either a multipurpose resume or another targeted resume.

Format and Layout. Gloria's resume is conservative in format and design, but it is innovative in the way it documents Gloria's abilities to perform the tasks required of a successful salesperson.

Summary. Gloria's resume does what she wants to do upon graduation. IT SELLS! Her resume is not a passive documentation of past experiences, but an active presentation of the abilities she has to succeed. The focus of her Professional Objective and the qualities projected in the Skills and Qualifications section reveal that Gloria knows what she wants and is prepared to go out and get it. She has shown that she can analyze a situation and the needs of a potential buyer, develop a market strategy, and make an effective presentation. She has done so with her resume!

GLORIA E. GLENN

School Address
14 Allenhurst
Norman, Oklahoma 73071
(405) 662-8877

Home Address
223 Chambless Drive
Beaumont, Texas 77705
(713) 236-8894

PROFESSIONAL OBJECTIVE

Position in computer hardware or software sales.

SKILLS AND QUALIFICATIONS

TECHNICAL KNOWLEDGE: Courses in calculus, statistics, computer science, and research techniques all utilized computer software programming and hardware. Knowledgeable of FORTRAN, Pascal, and SPSS. Wrote "Computers and College," a research paper exploring increased emphasis on computer-related courses and the development of computer usage skills in higher education. Developed database and retrieval program for alumni fund-raising efforts.

COMMUNICATIONS SKILLS: Numerous activities required developing ideas, organizing tasks, motivating people to accomplish goals, and delegating responsibility. Course work in sociology and psychology developed analytical perspective. Can communicate well one-on-one and in groups. Comfortable presenting ideas to large audiences.

SALES ABILITY: As campus leader, sold ideas and persuaded others to compromise or agree upon a common goal. As retail salesperson, developed sales-presentation skills and sales perspective. Confident of sales abilities. Profit-motivated.

EXTRACURRICULAR ACTIVITIES

GAMMA PHI BETA SORORITY, University of Oklahoma
Pledge Chairperson: Developed and implemented pledge training program for 45 pledges. (1989)
Panhellenic Delegate: As liaison between sorority and Panhellenic Council, worked with other sorority and fraternity representatives to promote and regulate the Panhellenic system. (1988–1989)

UNIVERSITY OF OKLAHOMA STUDENT FOUNDATION
Public Relations Committee: Promoted campus activities and events to students and alumni. (1988–1990)

UNIVERSITY OF OKLAHOMA ALUMNI ASSOCIATION
Computer Assistant: Developed database and retrieval system to identify alumni, note past contacts by Alumni Association, and note whether contributions were made. Used to increase effectiveness of fund-raising efforts. (1989)
Fund-raising Volunteer: Called alumni and solicited contributions during annual fund-raising drives. (1988–1990)

UNIVERSITY OF OKLAHOMA ADMISSIONS OFFICE
Tour Guide: Conducted tours for prospective students and their families. (1988–1990)

WORK EXPERIENCE

JEANS FOR US, Beaumont, Texas.
Salesperson: Assisted customers with selections, maintained inventory-control procedures, and assisted with buying and merchandise displays. (Summers 1985–1989)

JOSKE'S, Beaumont, Texas.
Salesperson: Assisted customers and operated cash register. (Part-time through high school)

EDUCATIONAL BACKGROUND

UNIVERSITY OF OKLAHOMA, Norman, Oklahoma.
Bachelor of Arts in Sociology, May 1990.
LAMAR UNIVERSITY, Beaumont, Texas. (1985–1986)

REFERENCES

A list of references will be provided upon request.

William S. Hanover:
An English Major's Presentation
Is Worth a Thousand Words

Special Features
- Activities given most significance for they most reflect qualifications
- Targeted resume with Objective statement that allows for options

---

The Problem. William S. Hanover, an English major, is a man of many talents. His academic pursuits trained him in written communications, his extracurricular activities throughout high school and college involved him in numerous publicity and promotional efforts, and he is an accomplished artist. *After thoroughly researching potential career fields, William concluded that either magazine or book publishing was the field that offered him the most flexibility and the best opportunity to use his many capabilities.* He wanted a resume that showed all of his talents, not one that focused on one or two.

The Solution. William created a resume that stresses the many extracurricular activities through which he developed publishing-related skills and that, by its design, illustrates his creativity. The resume begins with an Objective that refers to basic skill areas. This approach serves to set a skills-based tone, influencing a reader's review of the resume by presenting a skills analysis in the very beginning. The remainder of the resume describes the experiences that allowed William to develop these skills. William has developed writing and editing skills through his course work, his experiences as a legal assistant, and, above all, his work on numerous promotional materials. He has developed his abilities in design and illustration, as well as in promotions and advertising, through all of his extracurricular activities. These skills are the most important assets he has to offer, and his resume demonstrates that he has been very active in developing them.

Format and Layout. William selected a traditional approach in presenting his educational, extracurricular, and employment activities, and he connects experiences to skills through his cover letters. In fact, he formatted his cover letters in a creative way. After initial references to specific employers and positions, the body of the letter presents skills that parallel those that appear in the Objective, with relevant experiences appearing under each heading. The closing of each letter is as employer and job specific as the introduction.

Supporting Materials. William intends to distribute a portfolio containing samples of his work along with his resume. To personalize his portfolio, he decided to have his name and a creative yet conservative border printed on the cover. He also had the same border printed on the stationery he bought to use for cover letters. Both pieces are illustrated below.

Summary. The picture that the resume, portfolio, stationery, and cover letter paint is truly worth a thousand words. A job search package as creative as this one is sure to be effective.

Portfolio is created by folding 11-x-17 page like a book. Copies of selected works are placed in folder and sent with the resume to potential employers. Portfolio is printed on the same kind of paper used for the resume.

Stationery is created by printing border and heading on the same kind of paper used for the resume.

WILLIAM S. HANOVER

OBJECTIVE: Entry-level position in publishing using the following skills:
- Promotions
- Advertising
- Design
- Editing

EDUCATION: MIDDLEBURY COLLEGE, Middlebury, VT
Will graduate June 1990, with B.A. in English.
Dean's list, sophomore and junior years.
Strong background in studio art.
Fluent in French.
Computer programming knowledge of BASIC.

LA JOLLA HIGH SCHOOL, La Jolla, CA
Graduated June 1986 with Academic Distinction.
National Merit Letter of Commendation.

Activities included: Student Government Publicity Committee, Student Newspaper (received state recognition for my editorial cartoons), Speech and Debate, Drama Club. Designed school symbol.

MIDDLEBURY ACTIVITIES: ADVERTISING CLUB, *President and Founding Member:* Directed activities and coordinated projects of student organization established to publicize and promote services of college offices and on-campus events.

SEARCH COMMITTEE FOR DIRECTOR OF CAREER COUNSELING AND PLACEMENT, *Student Chairperson:* Chaired student interviewing committee and presented findings to Faculty and Administration Search committees.

ALUMNI-IN-RESIDENCE STEERING COMMITTEE, *Student Director:* Participated in review and selection of alumni to participate in week-long programs dealing with topical issues ranging from careers to the nuclear freeze movement.

MIDDLEBURY WINTER CARNIVAL COMMITTEE, *Member:* Designed T-shirt and publicity poster and assisted in planning and execution of all phases of annual event.

1989 CLASS COMMITTEE, *Member:* Planned and produced publicity for several campus events sponsored by committee to raise funds for class.

SIGMA PHI EPSILON, *Publicity Officer, Pledge Trainer, Assistant Rush Chairperson:* Promoted fraternity functions, planned rush and pledge activities, designed flyers for fraternity events. Elected "Most Valuable Brother," junior year.

EMPLOYMENT EXPERIENCE: WILMER, CUTLER AND PICKERING, Washington, DC
Legal Assistant/Librarian: Participated in research for several cases. Performed all aspects of case administration, including writing of preliminary briefs and interviewing of potential witnesses. Provided reference assistance to other legal assistants and attorneys and maintained law library. *Summer 1989*

BASKIN-ROBBINS 31 FLAVORS, La Jolla, CA
Waiter and Cashier. Summers 1988, 1987, and 1986

ADDRESSES:

Box 498	54 Hillside Drive
Middlebury College	La Jolla, CA 92037
Middlebury, VT 05753	619-455-9828
802-388-8747	(after June 30, 1990)

Lawrence Herder:
Many Years with Few Employers and Now Forced to Make a Change

---

Special Features
- Objective statement that leads into a summary of qualifications
- Targeted resume highlights qualifications for job change

The Problem. Lawrence Herder has had over twenty years of experience. For the past eight years, he has been the vice president of sales and marketing for an office-supplies and furniture distributor. When Lawrence left J.C. Penney to work for Offices Midwest, he was sure it would be his last job change. But when Offices Midwest was purchased by a larger company, Lawrence was asked to leave, even though he had held an important position within the company.

Lawrence first had to overcome some psychological and practical barriers before he could go back to job hunting. As someone who had not looked for a job in almost twenty years (Offices Midwest had come looking for him), Lawrence was rusty and unsure about how to proceed. Lawrence is a confident individual who has a long history of career success, but the prospect of job hunting can make the most secure individual anxious. After a great deal of thinking about why he had been successful in the jobs he had held in the past and what he wanted in the future, and after meeting several times with a career counselor, Lawrence developed some solid job search targets and dependable strategies. Lawrence came to realize along the way that he did not really want to go back to retailing or the office-supplies business. *After working through the many variables that confront career changers, Lawrence decided to look for a job in advertising sales with a television or radio station, but he was also interested in exploring other media-related sales and marketing positions.*

The Solution. Because the field of advertising sales was related to his previous jobs, Lawrence created a resume that ties his Objective statement together with a discussion of qualifications and past experiences. The summary of qualifications is joined to the statement of Objective; this technique helps Lawrence to convey to potential employers the fact that he is very much aware of his job search target and that he has the qualifications to perform the tasks associated with this job. The job descriptions appearing under the Employment heading highlight only general responsibilities because Lawrence did not want to appear to be "overqualified" and because he wanted potential employers to focus on his qualifications. Lawrence used his job search correspondence to detail specific responsibilities and accomplishments that supported his candidacy for a particular position. For his more open-ended search, Lawrence simply changed the Objective statement to read "Marketing and sales position that builds upon the following skills and experiences" and used cover letters to highlight related experiences and qualifications.

Format and Layout. Lawrence's resume combines the chronological and functional approaches. It has a statement of Objective that includes a summary of qualifications followed by an Employment section that presents Lawrence's work history in reverse chronological order.

Summary. Lawrence's story is that of a person who has had a successful career for many years and has been forced by circumstances to undertake a job search again. Having taken some time off to regroup and reevaluate his skills, Lawrence established new goals and came up with a new resume that effectively linked his qualifications to his new objective.

See Lawrence's job search success story on page 103.

Typeset in Optima. ➡

LAWRENCE HERDER

756 Buffalo Avenue
Chicago, Illinois 60617
(312) 263-8645

OBJECTIVE

Advertising sales position that builds on the following skills and experiences:
- *Over 20 years in sales-related capacities.*
- *Capable of making direct, person-to-person contact with agency media buyers and client advertising personnel.*
- *Knowledgeable of client perspectives and retail advertising strategies. Have dealt with advertising salespersons as Vice President of Sales and Marketing and Store Manager.*
- *Comfortable making group presentations, using quantitative data to support objectives. Can develop and use statistics as part of sales campaign. Have used personal computers.*
- *Academic background in communications.*

EMPLOYMENT

1982–present   **OFFICES MIDWEST,** Chicago, Illinois
VICE PRESIDENT OF SALES AND MARKETING
- *Responsible for all sales and marketing activities of office-supplies and furniture distributor with four retail outlets and sales force of 25. Manage direct contact, catalog, and retail sales efforts.*
- *Hire, train, and supervise all sales representatives and retail sales personnel.*
- *Create weekly newspaper advertisements and oversee publication of annual catalog and monthly sales brochures.*

1973–1982   **J.C. PENNEY CO. MIDWEST DIVISION,** Chicago, Illinois
STORE MANAGER–Evanston Mall Store (1978–1982)
- *Complete responsibilities for store operations.*
BUYER–Photographic Equipment and Office Supplies (1976–1978)
- *Buying and pricing responsibilities for 20 stores.*
MANAGEMENT TRAINEE (1973–1975)
- *Completed rotational program involving Department Manager, Assistant Buyer, and Assistant Store Manager positions.*

1970–1973   **GREAT WESTERN HOTELS,** Seattle, Washington
SALES REPRESENTATIVE/CONFERENCE COORDINATOR
- *Traveled throughout Midwest soliciting conference business for hotels in Great Western group.*
- *Made individual and group presentations, wrote contracts, and acted as liaison between client and hotels.*

EDUCATION

NORTHWESTERN UNIVERSITY, Evanston, Illinois
BACHELOR OF ARTS IN COMMUNICATIONS, 1968

Robert D. Jay:
Is Retail Really Right, Robert?

Special Features
- Targeted resume with statement of Objective
- Effective use of skills headings highlights diverse background

The Problem. With a major in psychology and a minor in computer science, Robert D. Jay had a varied academic background. He also had a wide range of extracurricular and employment experiences to his credit. By the time he graduated from college, he had worked in a bank, been an accounting tutor, represented a T-shirt printing company, and held almost every position possible with a college radio station.

When it came time for Robert to decide on his postgraduation employment goals, he had some difficulty. After doing a great deal of research—reading articles and books and interviewing alumni about their careers—*Robert decided that retail management offered the diversity he sought in a career field.* But, like many liberal arts job seekers, Robert did not want to "limit his possibilities," so, in addition to duplicating the targeted resume shown here, he produced an alternate—multipurpose—version by taking off the lead-in Objective statement.

The Solution. Because Robert had done so many different things, he decided it was important to present himself in as organized a fashion as possible. He created a fairly conservative resume but used skill headings to highlight his varied experiences.

A retailer reviewing this resume would probably regard Robert as a qualified candidate. Robert has had sales experience and is accomplished in the areas of finance, accounting, and basic management. And, beyond that, Robert has stated that he has a strong interest in retailing. The three Experience categories and the Computer Languages and Skills section all present information that would be of interest to employers in retailing and in numerous other industries as well.

Format and Layout. Robert's resume is intentionally conservative in its approach and presentation. It is typed and shows the use of capitalization for headings and underlining for job titles. The Computer Languages and Skills heading was placed at the bottom because of the importance of these skills in all fields. Robert included this heading in the hope that it would attract the attention of employers from several different industries.

See Robert's job search success story on page 105.

ROBERT D. JAY

University of Connecticut   269 Turkey Trot Lane
P.O. Box 367   Woodbridge, CT 06478
Storrs, CT 06268   (203) 794-3832
(203) 485-9868

OBJECTIVE
  Position in a retail management-training program.

EDUCATION
  UNIVERSITY OF CONNECTICUT, Storrs, CT.
  Candidate for B.A. degree, June 1990. Major in psychology. Minor in computer
  science. Course work in economics and accounting. Member of Kappa Kappa Kappa
  fraternity.

  AMITY REGIONAL SENIOR HIGH SCHOOL, Woodbridge, CT.
  Diploma received, June 1986. Scholastic honors for junior and senior years.

SALES AND PROMOTION EXPERIENCE
  EXPRESS YOURSELF, Storrs, CT.
  Campus Representative, fall 1989-spring 1990.
  Planned campus advertisements for professional silk-screening company that
  specializes in T-shirts and caps. Placed and delivered orders. Commission sales.

  WUCR, Storrs, CT.
  Promotions Director, spring 1988.
  Coordinated all promotional efforts of college radio station, including two large
  concert promotions and a fund-raising drive for the station.

  UNIVERSITY OF CONNECTICUT OFFICE OF ADMISSIONS, Storrs, CT.
  Tour Guide, spring 1988-spring 1990.
  Conducted informational tours for prospective students and families. Attended two
  Amity Regional Senior High School College Nights as University of Connecticut
  representative.

MANAGEMENT AND OFFICE EXPERIENCE
  UNIVERSITY OF CONNECTICUT CAREER CENTER, Storrs, CT.
  Student Assistant, fall 1989.
  Maintained complete listings of temporary and permanent jobs on computer
  database. Implemented data-manipulation software. Assisted in developing software
  to coordinate on-campus recruiting sign-up procedure. Counseled students seeking
  employment.

  WUCR, Storrs, CT.
  Served as Programming Director, Chief Announcer, Training Director, and
  Promotions Director for college radio station, spring 1987-spring 1990.

ACCOUNTING AND FINANCE EXPERIENCE
  UNIVERSITY OF CONNECTICUT DEPARTMENT OF ACCOUNTING, Storrs, CT.
  Tutor, spring and summer, 1989.
  Tutored and graded students in Introduction to Accounting. Responsibilities
  involved daily interaction with small groups and individual students.

  UNION TRUST COMPANY TAX DEPARTMENT, New Haven, CT.
  Tax Intern, spring 1988 and spring 1989.
  Assembled and proofread tax summaries and forms. Ensured that filing and payment
  deadlines were met. Worked independently.

COMPUTER LANGUAGES AND SKILLS
  Fluent in BASIC and PL/1. Knowledge of FORTRAN and Pascal. Experience with
  microcomputers and minicomputers as well as mainframe units.

Raymond Krieger:
An Art Major Who Does Not Want to Be Painted into a Corner

Special Feature
• Highlights experience, downplays art background

The Problem. Raymond Krieger majored in studio art but, after a very thorough and difficult self-assessment, he concluded that he did not have enough talent to be sure of a successful career in art. Not wanting to live out his days as a starving artist, and not wanting potential employers to perceive him as someone who is looking for a job only to pay the bills while pursuing an art career, Raymond created a decidedly business-oriented resume.

The Solution. Raymond was lucky enough to have had two exceptional work experiences while in school. He worked for a large employment agency full-time for three summers, part-time during the first two years of college, and when home on vacations from college. He also worked for a large retail department store part-time while in college and full-time one summer. These experiences both involved management-type responsibilities. *Since Raymond had enjoyed both jobs very much and since he had advanced in both organizations, he decided to capitalize on his experiences and seek employment in retail management or in human resources.*

Format and Layout. Raymond's resume lets his work experiences do most of the "talking." They are positioned prominently, taking up more space than any other entries, and are described in detail. A potential employer reading these descriptions must conclude that Raymond is a person who can manage people and tasks and accomplish objectives. Raymond did not want to use an Objective statement, because he felt he could draw attention to whichever experience was most relevant to the job he was applying for by means of a cover letter.

Although he was a studio art major, Raymond does not stress any of his art-related skills. In fact, he notes his major only in the last section of his resume. His greatest strengths are in fact the skills he acquired in his two long-term work experiences, and Raymond sells these strengths very effectively.

Summary. Raymond's resume highlights two very good work experiences and projects a person who can and will succeed in business. This art major will not be painted into a corner, and he will not be stereotyped. He will, however, be successful in his efforts to find a job that will get him started in a business career.

RAYMOND KRIEGER

3218 SE Woodstock Blvd.
Apartment 4
Portland, Oregon 97202
(503) 776-3195

182 Federal Ave.
Apartment 32B
Los Angeles, California 90045
(213) 823-6284

WORK EXPERIENCE

Personnel Counselor, Dynamic Personnel Resources, Inc., Los Angeles, CA
Interviewed applicants, initiated and developed employer contacts, visited client company operations, coordinated applicant and employer communications from initial contact to hiring. Specialized in clerical personnel.

Provided direct support for manager of clerical area—trained and supervised personnel counselors, maintained daily, weekly, and monthly individual and area performance records.
Summers 1986–1988 and part-time as needed 1986–1988

Assistant Buyer/Salesperson, I. Magnin, Portland, OR
Ordered merchandise, coordinated its arrival and transfer to departments, completed all paperwork involved in pricing and advertising, and supervised display of merchandise. Completed Junior Executive Training Program while full-time student. Promoted into program after six months as part-time salesperson.

As salesperson, assisted customers with selections, displayed merchandise, maintained inventory, and tabulated daily receipts.
Summer 1989 and part-time 1988–present

EXTRACURRICULAR ACTIVITIES

Fund-raising Volunteer, Reed College Development Office, Portland, OR
Solicited alumni donations via telephone fund-raising drives.   1988 and 1989

Kappa Sigma Fraternity, Reed College, Portland, OR
Publicity Chairman—Promoted fraternity events using posters and flyers. Designed and created all promotional materials. Coordinated decorations at various functions.   1987–1988

Greekspeak, Reed College, Portland, OR
Editor—Organized, edited, and coordinated production of newsletter for fraternities and sororities.
1986–1988

INTERESTS

Art
Sketch and paint landscapes and portraits.

Travel
Traveled throughout western United States, Mexico, and Spain. Speak Spanish.

EDUCATIONAL BACKGROUND

Reed College, Portland, OR
Bachelor of Arts in Studio Art, May 1990
Minor in English

Patricia M. Lansing:
A Scientist Seeks a Setting

Special Features
- Targeted resume without Objective statement
- Highlights scientific experiences with carefully selected headings and boldface type
- Used for job search, graduate school applications, and grant proposals

---

The Problem. *Patricia M. Lansing, a biology major, wanted to make use of her academic and extracurricular science activities to obtain an entry-level position with a scientific research organization, environmental protection organization, or laboratory.* She had done a great deal but had received only tuition credit or room and board for her efforts. Patricia did not receive an hourly wage or salary for any of the activities listed, but her aim was to present herself as a goal-oriented person with notable qualifications, not just as a science major with many volunteer experiences in her background.

The Solution. Patricia's resume reflects her desires clearly, but it does so without an Objective statement. The largest section is the one labeled Scientific Experience. Here Patricia discusses all of her science-related experiences. The question of whether she was paid for any of this work is irrelevant. Potential employers will see Patricia as a person qualified to work in research-oriented environments. They will have no doubts that she is experienced, and that is what is most important.

Patricia has clearly done more than laboratory work. She has done independent research, been involved in the research efforts of others, taught college and high school students, and gained computer programming capabilities. All of these qualifications are presented effectively on her resume.

In addition to forwarding her resume, Patricia provides each prospective employer with a copy of her transcripts and synopses of some of her research papers. This supplemental information will no doubt increase her chances of being selected. Liberal arts graduates seeking employment in scientific settings should expect to be asked to provide additional materials such as transcripts, synopses, and letters of recommendation. These documents can be submitted with the resume when first making contact with an employer or at a later time, perhaps after the interview.

The absence of an Objective statement allows Patricia to use her resume for purposes other than a job search. She may decide she wants to apply for admission to a doctoral program and for funding to continue her research. The resume she developed is an ideal vehicle for presenting her background to graduate schools and funding agencies; it presents much of the needed information in a concise and organized fashion. Having the resume at hand will allow Patricia to explore any of these options with very little extra effort.

Format and Layout. Patricia has developed a format that highlights her scientific experiences in various ways. As discussed, the largest section appears under the heading Scientific Experience. Patricia highlights the names of the organizations in each entry by having them set in capital letters. She sets off each activity in a similar way by using boldface type and having bullets set in front of each item. Potential employers reviewing this resume can quickly orient themselves and pick out related experiences. Patricia also uses boldface italics to highlight the summary statements that appear at the end of the Scientific Experience section.

PATRICIA M. LANSING

29 Campus Drive   *4 Agerton Road*
Durham, NC 27706   *Augusta, GA 30909*
Home: (919) 684-9729   *(404) 736-8726*
Office: (919) 684-3300

EDUCATION

DUKE UNIVERSITY   *Durham, NC*

- *A.B., June 1990*
- *Honors major in Biology   Overall GPA: 3.3   Biology GPA: 3.5*
- *Duke University Marching Band (1989–1990)*
- *Editor, Events Calendar (1989–1990)*
- *Delta Delta Delta Sorority (1987–1990)*

AUGUSTA SENIOR HIGH SCHOOL   *Augusta, GA*

- *Graduated 5th in class of 400, June 1986*
- *President, Biology Club (1984–1986)*
- *Nominated for Georgia Science Awards (1986)*

SCIENTIFIC EXPERIENCE

DUKE UNIVERSITY DEPARTMENT OF BIOLOGY   *Durham, NC*

- *Attended **Tropical Biology Study Program** in Puerto Rico (Summer 1989). Investigated aspects of terrestrial and marine ecology through lectures and field study. Originated hypotheses and researched and presented oral and written findings of group and individual projects.*
- *Received State of North Carolina grants to support **independent research on insect activities** (1988–1990). Designed and constructed original electronic equipment to quantify movement as related to temperature. Results used as a part of developing insect control strategy for Department of Agriculture.*
- ***Teaching Assistant** in Entomology (Summer 1988) and Botany (Spring 1987). Included laboratory instruction and field supervision, preparation and grading of examinations, and monitoring use of laboratory equipment.*
- ***Research Assistant** (1986–1988). Conducted chemical and biological experiments on pesticide potencies. Involved use of computers, sophisticated instruments, and advanced laboratory techniques.*

NATIONAL YOUTH SCIENCE CAMP   *Charleston, WV*

- ***Counselor** (Summer 1987). Taught seminars on botany and natural sciences.*
- *Selected as one of two students from Georgia to attend **six-week symposium on scientific topics** (Summer 1986). Chosen to return as counselor the following summer.*

UNITED STATES DEPARTMENT OF ENVIRONMENTAL PROTECTION   *Augusta, GA*

- ***Selected member of Youth Conservation Corps (Summer 1985). Improved trails and controlled erosion in state parks.***

Can program in BASIC and COBOL. Experienced in variety of laboratory techniques and use of laboratory equipment.

Judson Marks:
Excellent Experience, No Direction

Special Features
- Highlights skills to downplay lack of focus
- Detailed discussion of excellent work experiences
- Use of word processor allows for objectives to be added as needed
- Personalized stationery supplies graphic interest

The Problem. Judson Marks is a French major who has had excellent work experience yet lacks direction. He is unsure of what specific career field or job function would be right for him. After talking with a career counselor, assessing skills developed through previous work and extracurricular activities, and setting tentative job search targets, Judson still had a problem. *"I have narrowed down my areas of interest to six—international banking, marketing research, management information systems programming, manufacturing management, manufacturing purchasing, and consulting—but I can't narrow them down any further."* Having so many different career interests made it difficult for Judson to decide on what type of resume to use.

The Solution. To solve his problem, Judson decided it would be best to have his resume typed on a word processor so that he could quickly and easily change his Objective statement as needed. The sample resume printed here has no Objective. Not only can Judson add an Objective at a later date, he can revise the Skills Overview section to support the target job as stated in the Objective.

Most of Judson's resume is taken up by the Skills Overview and Work Experience sections. These two segments are the heart of his resume, for Judson's greatest assets come from the excellent experiences he has had over the summers. Judson first draws attention to the skills gained through these experiences, then provides detailed discussions of the responsibilities associated with each summer job. Judson also comments on the information that appears below these two major headings but does not go into quite as much detail.

Judson can change objectives and redirect the Skills Overview to prepare for directed communication with prospective employers in specific fields as needed. Rewriting a resume forces self-assessment and prompts continued research into potential job functions. Remember, the more you know about yourself and about the job you wish to have, the better you'll be able to communicate this knowledge in a resume, cover letter, or interview.

Format and Layout. Judson types his resume each time, using a personal computer with word processing software, with the particular Objective and Skills Overview he needs for the job he is interested in at the time. Judson decided to order his own paper and have his name printed boldly in the upper left-hand corner. This gives his resume a little flair and makes it easy to pick out. The body of the resume itself is laid out in a fairly traditional, conservative way, so that overall, the resume looks very businesslike. Judson gives only one address on his resume since using the word processor enables him to change the address as necessary before he has a new version printed out.

Summary. For a person with excellent experience but no real direction, this approach to resume writing is very effective. After Judson has done a little more research, he should be able to narrow down the possibilities a bit more. Six job search target fields are probably too much to handle, even for someone as experienced as Judson.

JUDSON MARKS
117 Skinker Boulevard
St. Louis, MO 63130
(314) 889-6620

SKILLS OVERVIEW

Capable of ***organizing and coordinating ideas as well as people and working toward specific goals.*** Can assess situations to develop and implement problem-solving strategies.

Capable of ***researching and analyzing information for practical use,*** such as writing a computer program to increase efficiency of information retrieval and deciding which contractors to use for major and minor repairs to fraternity house.

Trained and motivated people to achieve maximum performance in work and academic environments. Able to communicate and work with people of all ages and backgrounds.

As House Manager ***developed and utilized strong management, leadership, and decision-making abilities. Supervised members, administered budgets, and maintained facilities.***

As employee of Southwestern Bell was exposed to Marketing, Plant, and Revenue departments. Completed all assignments successfully. ***Developed special projects in addition to fulfilling responsibilities appearing on job descriptions.***

WORK EXPERIENCE

SOUTHWESTERN BELL TELEPHONE COMPANY, St. Louis, MO
Division of Revenues: Economic Analyst   Summer 1989
Collected information to write a computer program (BASIC) that analyzed revenues by departments and by weekly, monthly, and quarterly time periods. Supervised and instructed employees who entered data into system. Consulted with managers in other regional departments in order to gather data for study dealing with costs in Traffic Services Department. Prepared manual to instruct keypunchers on data input procedures for Traffic Services study. Presented results of study in a report to Division Manager and Division Vice President.

Plant Department: Summer Trainee   Summer 1988
Recorded and filed customer repair tickets. Updated repair equipment records. Entered customer repair data into computer.

Marketing Department: Summer Trainee   Summer 1987
Assisted in forecasting department budget. Compiled and analyzed studies on use of WATS systems by small businesses. Researched potential customers/companies for marketing purposes. Reviewed employee work schedules and devised vacation replacement schedules. Reorganized filing systems.

EDUCATION

WASHINGTON UNIVERSITY   St. Louis, MO
Bachelor of Arts, anticipated June 1990   Major: French
Overall GPA: 3.25/4.0

ACTIVITIES

PHI DELTA ALPHA FRATERNITY, Washington University
House Manager   1988–1990
Administered $5000 annual budget. Assigned rooms to members living in the house. Billed members for room and board expenses. Supervised two full-time staff persons and two student assistants. Attended house executive board meetings and decided upon issues related to the house. Had total control over all maintenance and repairs decisions and allocations.

Communications Chairman   1989–1990
Informed fraternity members of university and house events.

Intramural Chairman   1988–1989

INTRAMURAL DEPARTMENT, Washington University
Referee and Scorekeeper   1987–1989

PROJECT MOTIVATION, St. Louis, MO
Tutor and Counselor   1985–1987
Tutored and counseled underprivileged children in two inner-city elementary schools.

REFERENCES

Available upon request.

Randee Sue Stemmons:
The Newsworthy Psychology Major

Special Feature
• Skills and Abilities section used with Objective draws
   attention to Randee's capabilities, not her major

The Problem. Randee Sue Stemmons is one of many psychology majors who have no intentions of becoming a psychologist. *She wishes to find employment as a journalist, in either print or broadcast news,* but she has not majored in journalism and is aware she will be competing with students who have.

The Solution. To show potential employers the qualifications she has to meet the responsibilities of an entry-level position in journalism, Randee developed two different resumes. The first (page 82) is relatively traditional in format and content, while the second (page 83) is somewhat unusual, taking the form of a brief news piece. The second serves as both resume and writing sample.

Randee has had some experiences that were directly related to her job goals, and she naturally wanted to highlight them on her resume. To do so she included a Skills and Abilities section in her basic resume and discussed these attributes in more detail in her news-piece resume. Randee has had courses in journalism, technical writing, creative writing, and research techniques. These are highlighted in both resumes. Randee's on-air experience with her university's radio station was limited (she became involved in the station only after focusing on her job search target late in her senior year), but it was a valid experience and therefore appears in both resumes. Randee also cites experience she had with newspapers during her high school days, and, although it wasn't very extensive, it at least demonstrates her interest in the field of journalism.

Special Uses. Randee can use either resume alone, depending on the employer, or she can use them as a package. The news-piece resume is a bit unorthodox, and it could turn some conservative professionals off, but it is well written (Randee had a journalism professor assist her in developing the piece), and it presents her strengths in a forceful,

upbeat manner. Even if she doesn't use the news-piece resume for all job applications, she can use a great deal of its content in cover letters and during interviews. Randee also developed a small portfolio that includes some letters to the editor that had been published in her university newspaper, a few of the pieces she did for journalism and creative-writing classes, and some articles she wrote for her high school paper. In addition, Randee wrote a few samples of news copy about current events and had a tape recording made of her reporting the stories.

Format and Layout. Randee's basic resume highlights her focus and qualifications by means of the Objective statement and the Skills and Abilities section. The news piece incorporates techniques like italics to highlight "quoted sources." Both resumes were typeset and duplicated on high-quality paper to present a professional image.

Summary. Randee's resumes work for her because they project an image of someone who knows what will be expected of her in an entry-level position and who is confident of her ability to meet those expectations.

RANDEE SUE STEMMONS

Box 3987
University of North Texas
Denton, Texas 76203
(817) 563-2105

2323 Shady Glenn Drive
Apartment 1328-B
Dallas, Texas 75206
(214) 363-7643

OBJECTIVE

A position in the field of journalism involving research and reporting.

SKILLS AND ABILITIES

Strong written and verbal communication skills . . . on-air experience . . . command of research techniques required of journalistic and academic writing . . . course work in technical writing, creative writing, journalism, and research techniques . . . assertiveness . . . ability to work under pressure.

EDUCATION

University of North Texas, Denton, Texas.
Bachelor of Arts, December 1989. Major: Psychology. Minor: Art History.
Grade Point Average for the final three academic semesters: 3.75/4.0.
Dean's List: fall 1988, spring 1989, and fall 1989.

ACTIVITIES

KNTU, University of North Texas (fall 1989). Disc jockey for student radio station. Presented music programming and read hourly news reports.

DENTON SCHOOL FOR SPECIAL EDUCATION, Denton, Texas (summer 1989 and part-time 1988–present). Volunteer Counselor. Assist counseling staff to implement educational and therapeutic programs for children and adults.

RESIDENCE LIFE OFFICE, University of North Texas (fall 1987–present). Resident Assistant. Advise students on academic questions. Counsel students with personal problems. Act as liaison between students and Residence Life Office. Check students into dormitory rooms at the beginning of each semester and check students out of dormitory rooms at the end of each academic year. Take inventory of dormitories at the end of each academic year.

NTSU DAILY, University of North Texas (1986–present). Contributed numerous feature articles to student newspaper.

THE LION'S ROAR, Richardson High School, Richardson, Texas (1985–1986). Reporter. Contributed articles on various subjects. Specialized in sports.

REFERENCES

Richard C. Donner, Professor of English, (817) 563-2235.
Louise Ann Create, Professor of Psychology, (817) 563-2471.
Maryann McWhales, Director of Residence Life, (817) 563-5566.
(All are at the University of North Texas, Denton, Texas 76203.)

STUDENT SEEKS POSITION AS JOURNALIST

by Randee Sue Stemmons

After undertaking a thorough process of self-assessment and career research, Randee Sue Stemmons of 2323 Shady Glenn Drive, Apartment 1328-B, Dallas, Texas 75206, phone number (214) 363-7643, recently launched a determined effort to obtain employment in the field of journalism. Specifically, Ms. Stemmons is seeking a position involving research or reporting in broadcasting or newspaper journalism.

Randee will receive a Bachelor of Arts degree from the University of North Texas in Denton, Texas, in December 1989. A psychology major and art history minor, Randee expresses confidence that her academic, extracurricular, and employment experiences have provided the skills and motivation required to become a successful journalist. When questioned about specific skills and motivations, Stemmons said,

"My course work in psychology and art history has taught me how to express myself verbally and in writing. I can do the research required to prepare a story or article. I can analyze questions from a scientific, behavioral, or artistic perspective. I am intensely curious about how people feel and act—what makes them tick. I am assertive—if I want to know something, I'll ask questions and find answers. Pressure is an everyday thing at school. I constantly work under the pressure of deadlines, sometimes working 20-hour days on assignments."

Comparing her background to that of a journalism major, Stemmons remarked,

"I have taken Scientific and Technical Writing, Creative Writing, Research Techniques, and Introduction to Journalism: Basic Writing. My transcript may not have all of the course titles a journalism major has, but I have many of the skills that a journalism major has. I can write effectively in synopsis and prose forms. My psychology courses have provided me with training in interview techniques, and I have had some on-air experience at my school's radio station."

The past four years at UNT have been more than courses, examinations, and term papers for Randee. She was a member of the residence-life staff for three years, a volunteer at the Denton School for Special Education for the past two, and worked at the student radio station this fall. Learning by doing has been a theme in her education.

"I learned from all of my nonacademic experiences that listening and communicating are the keys to success. Listening allows someone to understand another person and the situation in which he or she is involved. Knowing how to translate listening into a written form is what journalism is all about. I have seen what listening and good communication can produce in an academic environment and in a therapeutic setting such as the school for special education. I want to share ideas and events with those who read printed media or with those who watch and listen to broadcast media."

Randee is well aware that a search for a position in the field of journalism will not be easy. She knows that there are only a few jobs and a great many job seekers and that only a select few are given opportunities to enter. Randee is a realist about her chances.

"I know it isn't going to be easy, especially since I majored in psychology and not in journalism or English, but I feel qualified and, most important, prepared. I have done a great deal of homework and thinking."

She is also optimistic about her chances for success.

"My commitment to finding a job is very strong. I am sure there is a person out there who will give me a chance to prove myself. I don't want to start out as an editor or on-air reporter. All I am looking for is an entry-level position. I want to proofread or write copy, research stories or articles, and assist in the production of stories. I want to have a chance to learn while I am performing what is expected of me. My portfolio may not be as full or sophisticated as a journalism major's, but it contains examples of the type of things I can do. It includes some of the articles I wrote for the Richardson High School newspaper, The Lion's Roar, *and some of the letters to the editor I had published in the NTSU* Daily. *I have also included some synopses of research papers I have written. All I want is a chance to show these to someone and an opportunity to explain why I want to be a journalist and how my experiences have prepared me to be a good journalist."*

Randee Stemmons is set on finding a job in journalism, and she asks for a chance. If determination and hard work are what make successful job seekers and successful journalists, Randee meets those requirements. *"She has been successful and will continue to be successful"* is what Richard C. Donner, Professor of English at the University of North Texas, (817) 563-2235; Louise Ann Create, Professor of Psychology, (817) 563-2471; and Maryann McWhales, Director of Residence Life, (817) 563-5566, echoed when questioned about Randee. Each of these individuals said that they would recommend her highly for positions in journalism and that they would welcome inquiries from employers seeking information about Randee's abilities.

If one believes what others say about Randee Sue Stemmons and what Randee has to say about herself, she will no doubt be an excellent journalist someday.

Howard M. Stevens: Ordinary Guy Does Not Want an Ordinary Resume

---

Special Features
- Traditional layout and graphics used to create professional image
- Internship heading highlights most important experience

The Problem. Howard M. Stevens, a social science major, thinks of himself as just an ordinary guy. Although Howard has had some interesting experiences, most notably an internship with a public television station, he did not have the confidence or enthusiasm required to create an effective resume or mount an aggressive job search. After receiving some simple suggestions from a career counselor concerning ways to highlight important information on his resume, Howard seemed to perk up. The resume Howard devised not only illustrates a good approach to resume writing, but it also reflects his growing self-confidence.

If Howard receives additional career counseling focused on researching potential career fields, he will become even more confident of his abilities and of his qualifications for employment. With a job goal in mind, Howard can rework the resume by adding an Objective statement and, perhaps, some form of summary of skills. For now, the resume as it appears can be used for many purposes—for researching employment opportunities by means of informational interviews as well as for applying for specific jobs.

The Solution. Howard was at first concerned that he wouldn't be able to fill up a page with pertinent information. After being told by a counselor that it is not the length of the resume but the content, the format, and, most important, what one does with the resume that count, Howard relaxed and was finally able to write a very good first draft. In this draft Howard highlighted what he believed was his most important experience while in school (next to playing varsity basketball!). This was his internship with a public television station. He placed this entry in a prominent position and used a special heading to make it stand out.

Initial career research, including a number of informational interviews, has led Howard to consider applying for jobs as a researcher with a federal, city, or state agency; with an elected official; or with a television or radio station. Howard came to realize that his internship experience and course work provided him with a background that could be applied in any of these target fields. He therefore styled his resume to attract the attention of employers in these specific areas.

Format and Layout. Howard's resume is very traditional in its appearance and layout. It uses basic headings to present experiences and capitalization to highlight major headings. Liberal spacing was used between separate elements of the resume to make the document appear a bit fuller than it really is, and typesetting was chosen to project a very businesslike image. Howard used matching stationery and envelopes to create a thoroughly professional presentation.

Summary. Howard sought the advice of professional career counselors, which resulted in his being able to zero in on several job-target fields that have real potential for him. He is very pleased with his resume—finally having a completed document in hand seems to have made life a lot easier—and he is now very optimistic about his chances for success. Howard is not really as ordinary as he thought. He had been suffering from the lack of self-confidence that too many liberal arts graduates have at first, but with this resume he has taken a first step, a major step, toward job search success.

HOWARD M. STEVENS ───────────────────────

Creighton University
P.O. Box 239
Omaha, Nebraska 68178
(402) 448-7895

EDUCATION

Creighton University, Omaha, Nebraska.
Bachelor of Arts in Social Science, expected May 1990.

Course work included: Legislative Process, Sociological Research Techniques,
Practical Electoral Politics, The Media and the Law, Introduction to Journalism.

INTERNSHIP

Nebraska Public Television, spring and fall 1989.
Researched information for investigative report on housing discrimination in Lincoln and
Omaha as part of social science and political science courses.
Did voice-overs for portions of production. Wrote term paper on issues of media's impact on
legislative process.

ACTIVITIES

Creighton University Varsity Basketball, 1986-1990.

Kappa Kappa Kappa Fraternity, 1987-1990.

Nebraska Public Television, 1989-1990.
Answered phones during membership and fund-raising drives.

Political Campaigns, 1988.
Campaigned door-to-door and on the telephone for congressional and gubernatorial
candidates.

EXPERIENCE

Omaha Credit and Collection Agency, summers, 1989 and 1987.
Collected overdue installment accounts and counseled customers on suitable
repayment plans.

Creighton University Athletic Department, part-time 1988-1990.
Opened and closed gym and maintained locker room areas.

Creighton University Alumni Memorial Library, summer 1988.
Checked out and restacked books.

REFERENCES

A placement file, including letters of recommendation, is available upon request from the
Creighton University Office of Career Planning and Placement, Lower Becker Hall, Room 38,
Omaha, Nebraska 68178.

Jay B. Stuart:
Pre-Med Retread—Life After Rejection

> **Special Features**
> - Basic resume for variety of job search options
> - Can be used for reapplication to med school

The Problem. Jay B. Stuart was a chemistry major who applied to medical school and didn't get in. He had good grades (a 3.0 GPA) and strong work and extracurricular experiences, but he didn't have exactly what the schools he applied to were looking for. After dealing with the emotional effects of rejection and coming to terms with the fact that he had to explore other options, Jay sought the assistance of his professors and a career counselor. *After digesting all of the advice he received and doing a great deal of soul-searching, Jay decided that he would do something related to the field of medicine for a year or two and then reapply to medical school.* Because Jay was realistic enough to know that he might not be admitted to med school when he reapplied and because he wanted to consider workable alternative careers, he decided to start his first job hunt with a broad, multipurpose resume.

The Solution. Because the number of possible careers in medicine and health-related fields is so large, Jay felt most comfortable with a resume that did not have an Objective statement. He wanted to be able to stress his particular strengths, as appropriate, in cover letters or during interviews. For example, if he were applying for a laboratory job, he would include in his letter details about the many lab courses he had taken and highlight the laboratory techniques he was familiar with. For positions in hospital administration or patient services, Jay might choose to elaborate on the administrative and organizational skills he included under the Activities heading.

Jay's academic, extracurricular, and employment experiences have left him with some very valuable skills. Because he is unsure about how and where he might apply these skills and because he wants to keep his option open, Jay prefers a resume that could be used to apply for jobs in a number of different medical and health-related fields.

Special Uses. Jay's resume is a very good basic document that can be reworked in a number of ways. If Jay does reapply to medical school, an updated version of the resume, stressing scientific course work and research experience, could be used to support his candidacy. If continued exploration of careers leads Jay to seek jobs outside of the field of medicine, his resume could easily be reworked to emphasize general skills.

Format and Layout. Jay chose traditional major headings and a chronological listing, using his personal computer to develop his resume and his laser printer for the final copy. It presents a very good image and is appropriate for the variety of employers that Jay will contact.

Summary. After having invested so much time and energy and emotion in applying to medical school and being rejected, Jay wants to redirect his efforts at obtaining the very best alternative job possible. Although unsure of exactly what this job will be, he is undertaking all of the activities required to gain focus and carry out a successful job search. For this pre-med retread, life after med school rejection will be successful.

JAY B. STUART

Present Address
3264 Maple
Clinton, New York 13323
(315) 853-9753

Home Address
48 Dix Hills Road
Dix Hills, New York 11746
(516) 644-8639

EDUCATION

Hamilton College, Clinton, NY
Candidate for A.B., June 1990
Chemistry major

Additional course work in economics, statistics, computer science (BASIC), and psychology

Half Hollow Hills High School West, Dix Hills, NY
Graduated June 1986, top 10% of the class

ACTIVITIES

Hamilton College Community Services Committee
Governing Board (1987-1989)
Carried out administrative functions of organization. Developed budget proposal, presented budget request to administration, and administered approved budget.

Big Brother/Big Sister Program (1987-1990)
Cochairperson (1989-1990)
Organized program-wide events, recruited new members, and matched pairs.
Big Brother to local underprivileged youth (1987-1990)

Sigma Nu Fraternity (1987-1990)

Half Hollow Hills Blood Drive
Coordinator (1984-1986)
Chaired committee that administered school blood drives. Selected sites, recruited donors, and handled relations with Red Cross.

WORK EXPERIENCE

Lenox Hill Hospital, New York, NY
Supervisor, Summer Youth Employment Program (summer 1989)
Supervised forty youths who served as volunteers in all areas of hospital, including emergency room, pharmacy, and wards. Assigned weekly responsibilities, oversaw completion of assignments, interacted with hospital staff and administration, and dealt with concerns of program participants.

University of Southern California Medical School, Los Angeles, CA
Research Assistant (summer 1988)
Carried out neurophysiological experiments on animals. Analyzed data and did library research. Proofread manuscripts.

Camp Merrimac, Contoocook, NH
Lifeguard and counselor (summers 1987 and 1986)

Lois Timstead:
Vita to Resume:
Rejecting a Gypsy Scholar's Life

Special Features
- A functional resume for a job search outside of academia
- Skills and Qualifications section, appearing first, highlights greatest strengths

---

The Problem. After more than seventeen years in higher education—eight as a student and over ten as a full-time teacher—Lois Timstead decided it was time to seek opportunities outside of academia. To do this, she first of all had to change her curriculum vitae into a resume.

Lois had prepared herself for life as a college professor. After completing work for a Ph.D. from Cornell, Lois received an appointment at SUNY Binghamton. She was delighted to be working in New York State and dreamed of being granted tenure and staying forever. Forever turned out to be only three years, however. Denied an advancement, Lois decided to move to Oregon for a change of life-style and climate. The climate was indeed different, but her working life-style was too much the same. Having been unable to obtain an appointment at the University of Oregon, Lois settled for a position on the faculty of a community college. Sometime later, Lois was finally granted a position as visiting lecturer at the University of Oregon. After fulfilling the responsibilities of both jobs for several months, Lois began to think about whether she wanted to work this hard, continuing down a path she had walked before without any assurances that it would lead to the security she sought. But as an ex-teacher and a Ph.D. who could not find tenure, Lois was not certain she could present herself to an employer as someone worth hiring.

The Solution. After Lois sat down and worked on a skills inventory and flowchart and functional resume, she realized that she really did have a great deal to offer potential employers. Lois decided to start searching for opportunities to use her foreign-language skills and knowledge of foreign countries and cultures. *Lois was soon confident that her talents could be applied to the business world,* *and she became convinced that her skills as a free-lance translator and interpreter were marketable ones.*

Format and Layout. Lois chose to write a functional resume to replace her curriculum vitae and to highlight her skills. A curriculum vitae, sometimes called a "vita" or "c.v.," is a complete and thorough documentation of all academic experiences; it normally includes listings of education and employment, publications and presentations, and involvements in associations and committees. The resume is a briefer, more functional document used to communicate with nonacademic employers.

Lois had her resume typeset to project a businesslike image. She had earlier used a chronological approach on her vita but found it would be more effective to use a functional approach on her resume, to both downplay her academic past and highlight the skills she has to offer. The Skills and Qualifications section sets the tone of the resume and presents Lois as a person who has much to offer an organization involved in international business. Note that Lois summarized her teaching and writing experience and elaborated on her free-lance translating and interpreting and her involvement on various committees.

Summary. Having decided she does not want the life of a gypsy scholar, Lois developed a resume that can be used to help her find the security as well as the challenges and rewards she seeks. Using this functional, efficient resume, Lois should have no trouble finding an excellent job outside of the academic world.

LOIS TIMSTEAD

53 Arrowsmith Road
Eugene, Oregon 97402

Home (503) 686-3221
Work (503) 686-3558

SKILLS AND QUALIFICATIONS

FLUENT IN SPANISH AND PORTUGUESE, CONVERSANT IN ITALIAN.
- Can translate business documents, reports, and correspondence.
- Can interpret for individuals or groups.
- Can develop written materials—brochures, advertisements, reports, and letters.
- Can teach introductory, intermediate, and advanced levels of conversation to individuals or groups.

KNOWLEDGEABLE OF FOREIGN COUNTRIES, CULTURES, AND POLITICAL SYSTEMS.
- Can coordinate travel arrangements to foreign countries; special knowledge of Central America, South America, Mexico, and the Caribbean.
- Can act as guide for individuals or groups traveling to foreign countries and as host to foreign visitors.
- Can educate individuals involved in international business about cultural and political issues.

EXPERIENCED IN COORDINATING EVENTS AND WORKING WITH COMMITTEES.
- Can develop strategies to reach goals.
- Can coordinate all aspects of meetings and conferences.
- Can make decisions, delegate responsibility, and supervise and judge the performance of others.

EXPERIENCE

FREE-LANCE TRANSLATOR AND INTERPRETER   1979–present
Have translated business documents and personal correspondence and have served as interpreter for numerous individuals and groups. Clients have included banks, travel agencies, manufacturers, retail stores, and social service agencies.

TEACHER AND WRITER   1980–present
Have taught Spanish and Portuguese language and literature at the University of Oregon (1989–present); Lane Community College (1987–present); State University of New York at Binghamton (1984–1987); and Cornell University (1980–1984). Have edited a textbook and written numerous articles.

EDUCATION

CORNELL UNIVERSITY, Ithaca, New York   1978–1984
Ph.D. Major Field: 20th-century Spanish-American literature.

UNIVERSITY OF WISCONSIN–MADISON, Madison, Wisconsin   1977–1978
M.A. Concentration: Ibero-American Studies. Minor: Portuguese.

STATE UNIVERSITY OF NEW YORK AT ALBANY, Albany, New York   1973–1977
B.A. Major: Latin American Studies. Minor: Spanish literature and language.

COMMITTEES AND ACTIVITIES

EXECUTIVE COMMITTEE OF ASSOCIATION OF CARIBBEAN STUDIES   1984–1986
Coordinated travel arrangements and accommodations for conferences in Havana, Cuba, and in Nassau, Bahamas. Was responsible for securing facilities and supervising efforts of others at conference sites as well as negotiating with government officials. Each conference lasted four days and involved over 300 participants.

EXECUTIVE COMMITTEE OF THE FACULTY   1985–1986
Elected to serve on committee dealing with various academic and administrative issues, including tenure and curriculum, at State University of New York at Binghamton.

FACULTY COMMITTEE ON ADMISSIONS   1984–1986
Served on committee involved in admissions process at State University of New York at Binghamton.

REFERENCES

Available upon request.

Carol P. Wallace:
Leaving the Mental Health Field
for Peace of Mind

Special Features
- Objective highlights skills that are transferable from one field to another
- Resume shows the value of a mental health worker to business employer

---

The Problem. An undergraduate psychology major and holder of a Master of Arts degree in social and organizational psychology, Carol P. Wallace wants and needs a change. After working in a mental health setting for ten years, Carol is suffering from burnout. She wants to enter the business world to obtain such tangible rewards as money and steady advancement, but she is not exactly sure where she wants to work or in what capacity. Carol is absolutely certain she wants to make a change and can discuss for hours the reasons she is tired of working within the stressful environment of a psychiatric treatment facility. She feels she must make a change for her own peace of mind.

The Solution. Carol decided she needed a resume that would project her motivation and her considerable skills (not her emotions!) to a potential employer. In order to decide which experiences to list, she began by making a careful assessment of skills. A review of her academic and employment experiences revealed several clearly definable skills areas that would be of interest to potential employers. Carol highlights these areas at the very beginning of the resume under the heading Professional Objective, detailing her skills in three separate paragraphs labeled Management, Research and Evaluation, and Human Resources and Counseling. *Carol can use this resume effectively to respond to advertisements for specific job openings or to present to potential career advisers when requesting an informational interview.*

By going through the process of assessing her skills and interests, which is required of anyone who hopes to write an effective resume, Carol gained a greater awareness of the qualities she has to offer an employer. Having completed the resume, she now feels that her job search has really begun. Carol can now go from talking about looking for a new job to taking action—to taking real steps toward her goal. As her job search continues and as increased knowledge of potential career fields results in more clearly focused job targets, Carol can revise her resume by changing the Professional Objective—by replacing "business setting" with the name of the specific field or job she seeks—and by rephrasing the skill areas to reflect knowledge of the skills required for that specific field or job.

Format and Layout. Carol's resume presents a person who has nothing to hide. She presents her academic background and experience, which are very much slanted to mental health/psychology-related areas. She also communicates the fact that she is now ready to apply her skills in other fields, and she projects her potential to employers by means of the Professional Objective section at the head of the resume.

Summary. Carol's resume will help her make the transition from her present field of employment to another. Completing the resume was the first of many job search activities that transformed Carol into a dynamic job seeker who catches the attention of employers in a wide range of fields. The fact that Carol is able to present her qualifications in terms of three skills areas rather than in terms of field-specific work experiences alone allows her to try her resume out on recruiters from several different industries. Carol has a great deal more to do before her job search will end, but her resume has gotten her off to a very good start.

CAROL P. WALLACE

38 Calle Buena
Tucson, Arizona 85715
(602) 625-0735

PROFESSIONAL OBJECTIVE

A position in a business setting utilizing the following skills:

MANAGEMENT - Supervisory responsibilities at Shadylawn involve management of staff, including scheduling, making evaluations, and hiring. Monitor use of all facilities and equipment and maintain detailed records.

RESEARCH AND EVALUATION - Course work in statistics, math, research design, and psychological testing. Completed master's thesis involving original hypothesis and research design. Gained experience in test administration and interpretation at Arizona Rehabilitation Commission. At Shadylawn develop written treatment plans for patients and maintain progress records.

HUMAN RESOURCES AND COUNSELING - Major academic training in psychology. All paid professional experiences involved working in a psychological services capacity. Have developed individual and group counseling skills. Capable of motivating staff to carry out treatment plans and maintaining high morale in stressful settings. While at Tucson Community College gained experience in academic and vocational counseling and cotaught a workshop for career changers.

EXPERIENCE

SHADYLAWN PSYCHIATRIC HOSPITAL, Tucson, AZ

Area Supervisor/Mental Health Worker—January 1983–present.

Psychiatric Aide—June 1981–January 1983.

TUCSON COMMUNITY COLLEGE, Tucson, AZ

Counseling Center Intern—September 1981–June 1982, part-time while student.

ARIZONA REHABILITATION COMMISSION

Psychological Assistant—December 1980–May 1981.

EDUCATION

UNIVERSITY OF ARIZONA, Tucson, AZ

Master of Arts—Social and Organizational Psychology, August 1982.
Emphasis on deviant behavior, counseling techniques, theories of social psychology, and research methods. Cumulative Grade Point Average: 3.4/4.0.

Bachelor of Arts—Psychology, June 1980.
Emphasis on experimental psychology and research design.
Minor, Sociology. Cumulative Grade Point Average: 3.3/4.0.

REFERENCES

References, including letters of recommendation, are available upon request.

Nell Woodward:
A Major and a Resume, Both Visual Studies

Special Features
- A targeted resume that demonstrates the creativity that is associated with Nell's job search goal
- Unique format and graphics

The Problem. Nell Woodward knew from the time she chose her major—visual studies—that she wanted to pursue a career in architecture. Tired of academics at the end of her senior year, Nell decided that she would rather get some practical training than go right on to a master's program in architecture. Because she had no directly related experiences other than academic course work and a job in the art library, Nell decided that a few years in the field, working in drafting or in some other entry-level capacity, was what she needed.

The Solution. *Nell therefore set her sights on an entry-level position with an architectural firm.* She created a resume that would attract the attention of potential employers because of its unique format and graphics. Both the content and the format of Nell's resume communicate her goals to potential employers: her Objective statement tells them exactly what she wants to do, and the resume's creative design and layout demonstrate something of her artistic talents.

Format and Layout. Nell decided to have her resume typeset, using a bold, artistic type style for major headings and a more conservative style for the content. When Nell sends her resume to employers she folds it like a flier, revealing her name and a statement similar to the resume's Objective on the cover, which is actually the reverse side of the resume. When the flier is opened the contents of the resume are revealed, including another presentation of identifying information and objective.

Summary. Nell's resume would not be appropriate for a position with a bank, but it is very well suited to the fields Nell is interested in. It presents information clearly and at the same time demonstrates her artistic style and design abilities.

NELL WOODWARD
IS SEEKING
AN ENTRY-LEVEL
POSITION WITH AN
ARCHITECTURAL FIRM

Typeset in Optima (desktop publishing program). ➡

NELL WOODWARD

Box 345
University of Massachusetts at Amherst
Amherst, MA 01003
(413) 545-8635

34 King Arthur Court
Palo Alto, CA 94303
(415) 322-5445

OBJECTIVE

Entry-level position with an architectural firm using education and experience in architecture and visual studies.

EMPLOYMENT

YOUTH ENTERPRISES   Palo Alto, CA
Supervisor/Manager, January 1989–March 1989.
   Supervised a group of high school students involved in recycling project. Responsible for accounts management
   and all public relations efforts.
GEMCO STORES   Mountain View, CA
Sales Clerk, September 1988–December 1988.
   Performed sales, cashier, and stock duties. Ordered and maintained inventory for two departments of large retail
   department store.

EDUCATION

UNIVERSITY OF MASSACHUSETTS AT AMHERST   Amherst, MA
Candidate for B.A., June 1990.
Major: Visual Studies with concentration in Architecture.
Course work in History of Architecture, Architectural Design, Urban Design, Computer Graphics, Physics,
   Engineering, and Drawing.
Activities: Director of Student Advertising Committee
          Member of Equestrian Team
          Participant in Foreign Study Program in Florence, Italy
          Freshman Adviser
UNIVERSITY LIBRARY, University of Massachusetts at Amherst   Amherst, MA
Student Assistant to Art Librarian, September 1986–June 1990.
Responsible for circulation of all art journals and reserve materials and in-depth research for professors in Art
Department.

PORTFOLIO AND REFERENCES

Complete portfolio of works and a list of references are available upon request.

Stacey York:
The Past and Future Journalist, Perhaps

Special Features
- Two resumes used to expand job search possibilities
- Chronological and functional resumes allow a job seeker with strong experiences in particular fields to present herself as well rounded and flexible

---

The Problem. An English literature major and psychology minor, Stacey York is a person who seems to have done it all, but she is unsure of what she wants to do next. Much of her past extracurricular, academic, and work experience has been related to journalism, yet she is not convinced that she would like her first postgraduation job to be in journalism. Research of potential entry-level opportunities expanded her list of tentative job targets to include a number of fields outside of communications. *Stacey decided she would like to interview for jobs in the following areas: advertising, broadcasting, consulting, book publishing, and magazine publishing; she also thinks she might enjoy writing speeches and/or doing administrative work for a Congressman or Senator.*

The Solution. Because she does in fact have a great deal to offer, Stacey can afford to approach the job hunt with a "grocery-store mentality" and shop around from employer to employer for a while. Because she did not want to keep track of six different resumes, Stacey developed two resumes that could communicate many things to many different employers.

Format and Layout. The use of a chronological resume and a functional resume titled Summary of Skills gives Stacey the flexibility she needs for her multidirectional job search. Both resumes effectively document many of her past experiences. Refer to Stacey's Chronological Flowchart on pages 17 to 21 and note that Stacey chose to document different experiences on each resume; she did not include everything on both.

Stacey felt that her chronological resume would not best present the breadth of her skills and experiences to employers in fields other than retailing or communications, so she created a functional resume to use in other instances. The functional resume best presents the broad range of skills that Stacey has to offer.

Special Uses. Stacey could, if she wishes, develop supplemental pages with summaries of skills for each of her job goals and then create targeted functional resumes with stated objectives. This would allow her to highlight field-specific skills and use headings that do not appear on her general Summary of Skills. Specific skills identified in Stacey's Skills Flowchart (pages 31 and 32) and Job Target Chart (pages 41 and 42) could be highlighted as appropriate on the targeted functional resumes.

Summary. Both versions of Stacey's resume communicate the fact that she is accomplished in many different areas; the arrangement of the information and the professional layout of the resumes testify to the fact that Stacey is a person who can make an attractive and effective presentation. Stacey's resumes give the clear impression that she will be able to apply her multidimensional talents—her liberal arts power—to any challenge placed before her and that she will succeed!

STACEY YORK

Stanford University
Post Office Box 783
Stanford, California 94305
(415) 498-8362

349 Ridgewood Road
Maplewood, New Jersey 07040
(201) 763-5894

EDUCATION

STANFORD UNIVERSITY, Stanford, CA
Candidate for A.B. degree in June 1990.
GPA as of fall 1989 3.2 (out of a possible 4.0).
Major in English literature. Minor in psychology.

Participated in Stanford-in-France Program in Nice, France.
Member of Stanford Women's Crew. Editor *Stanford Crew Notes.*
Member of Alpha Chi Omega Sorority. Rush Co-Chairwoman and Panhellenic Society
Representative. Reporter for *The Stanford Daily* student newspaper.

COLUMBIA HIGH SCHOOL, Maplewood, NJ
Graduated in June 1986.
Ranked in top 10% of class.

National Honor Society.
Junior Class Secretary.
Editor of yearbook.

EXPERIENCE

STANFORD SPORTS INFORMATION OFFICE, Stanford, CA
Administrative Intern, spring 1988 to present.
Reported on all Stanford sports events. Managed postgame football press-box operations for
Stanford games and for East-West Shrine games. Published feature stories about Stanford athletes.
Assisted in development of press guides and programs. Wrote press releases.

Football Statistician, fall 1989 and fall 1988.
Compiled statistics. Wrote game summaries and weekly reports.

MOBIL OIL CORPORATION, New York, NY
Public Relations Intern, summer 1989.
Researched information for Mobil's Op-Ed advertisements, "Observations" columns, and special
publications. Proofread copy and checked facts. Replied to reader correspondence. Coordinated
Mobil School Visitation Program.

PALO ALTO HILTON INN, Palo Alto, CA
Hostess and Waitress, summer 1988.

MACY'S DEPARTMENT STORE, Livingston, NJ
Salesperson, winter 1988 and summer 1987.

Supervisor/Salesperson, fall 1984 to summer 1986.
Supervised salespeople, completed nightly closings, and maintained various departments in
manager's absence. Rotated throughout store as needed. Youngest supervisor in store.

INTERESTS

Enjoy playing the piano and guitar, oil and acrylic painting. Avid bicyclist. Have traveled in Europe
and throughout the western United States.

REFERENCES AVAILABLE UPON REQUEST.

SUMMARY OF SKILLS OF STACEY YORK

Stanford University
Post Office Box 783
Stanford, California 94305
(415) 498-8362

349 Ridgewood Road
Maplewood, New Jersey 07040
(201) 763-5894

OBJECTIVE   A position utilizing the skills acquired in the experiences outlined below.

WRITING
- Reported on sports events for *The Stanford Daily.*
- Published feature stories for Stanford athletic programs and Bay Area newspapers.
- Currently working on a novel for independent study English course.

Samples of work available upon request.

RESEARCH
- Researched Mobil Oil Corporation's Op-Ed advertisements, "Observations" columns, and special publications.
- Updated statistical information for Stanford University football brochures and programs.
- Initiated independent study survey of students' opinions of the Stanford Honor Code. Presented results in videotape presentation.
- Conducted survey of passengers using Stanford shuttle bus system utilizing on-the-spot interviewing and questionnaires.

ORGANIZATION AND MANAGEMENT
- Edited *Stanford Crew Notes.* In charge of copy, layout, and circulation for monthly publication dealing with men's and women's crew.
- Student Liaison Officer for Stanford Alumni Club of Northern New Jersey. Coordinated activities for prospective students from northern New Jersey at Alumni Club events. Represented Stanford at college nights. Corresponded with applicants from northern New Jersey. Greeted and hosted visitors from northern New Jersey during stays at Stanford.
- Supervised salespeople and managed various departments as supervisor/salesperson at Macy's department store.
- Coordinated visits of over 25 schools (over 2,000 students) to Mobil Oil Corporation's world headquarters for Mobil's School Visitation Program.

CREATIVITY
- Studied piano for 10 years; additional training in guitar and voice.
- Performed in high school dramatic productions.
- Paint with oils and acrylics.

EDUCATION   STANFORD UNIVERSITY, A.B., June 1990
Major: English literature. Minor: psychology. GPA: 3.2/4.0.

EXPERIENCE   STANFORD SPORTS INFORMATION OFFICE, Administrative Intern (spring 1988–present),
    Football Statistician (fall 1989 and fall 1988).
MOBIL OIL CORPORATION, Public Relations Intern (summer 1989).
PALO ALTO HILTON INN, Hostess and Waitress (summer 1988).
MACY'S DEPARTMENT STORE, Salesperson (winter 1988 and summer 1987),
    Supervisor/Salesperson (fall 1984–summer 1986).

Job Search Success Stories

Jordan Elizabeth Alna

A revised resume puts this biology major in business with a health-care sales position.

Once she revised her resume and, in a sense, revived her job search, Jordan showed initiative and courage by taking a few steps back to make several leaps forward. First, she spent more time with the recruiter who suggested she change her resume. This person, a representative of a large pharmaceutical firm, clarified for Jordan subtle distinctions between organizations in the field, suggested people for employment and informational interviews in pharmaceutical firms and hospitals, and taught Jordan a sales-oriented approach to following up contacts. Then, she followed up with all of the other recruiters she had met. Using the revised resume and more goal-directed letters (see samples on pages 137 and 138) as appropriate reasons for renewing communications, she asked for feedback concerning her candidacy, if she could be granted additional consideration, and for suggestions concerning next steps. When appropriate, if Jordan felt her relationship was strong enough or if she felt she was no longer under consideration by a specific organization, she asked the recruiter for some referrals to similar organizations. Through this networking she was able to revitalize and expand her health-care-related search.

In addition to referrals, Jordan used professional association directories and phone surveying to identify public relations personnel for hospitals within geographic areas of interest. Like many college seniors, Jordan wished to explore opportunities in Ohio, near her soon-to-be alma mater, and near home in Little Rock. Thus, she developed clearly defined geographic goals, job search goals, and increasingly powerful job search tools and, most important, attitudes. Because she had begun her efforts early in the fall of her senior year, Jordan still had the time to be a persistent and patient, yet powerful, liberal arts job seeker.

Jordan's residence life and secondary teaching searches were a bit more straightforward. Through her university's career services office, Jordan was made aware of postings that appeared weekly in *The Chronicle of Higher Education,* and she was able to develop a hit list of schools where she might like to work and the appropriate deans or directors to contact. She was also counseled concerning the use of "search firms," which specialize in secondary school teacher placement, and she developed a listing of private secondary schools where she would direct her self-initiated efforts. While Jordan was appropriately assertive and creative, these searches involved the more traditional application process with deadlines and time frames for interviewing. Therefore, she was able to direct more of her energies to the demands of the more unpredictable health-care-related search.

While it is unrealistic for most college job seekers to expect that they will have offers and make decisions by graduation, Jordan proved to be an exception to this rule. A great deal of pre-search activity during the fall and early winter and job search activity throughout the spring months, including winter and spring breaks, proved successful. As of early June, Jordan received offers to teach at a private secondary school in Little Rock, to stay at Denison as a Residence Hall Coordinator, and to enter the sales-management program of a major manufacturer of health-care products and equipment. Ironically, but not unexpectedly if one believes in liberal arts power, this last offer came from an organization that had rejected Jordan after an initial on-campus interview.

All job seekers wish to obtain as many offers as possible before they make their decision, but reality does not often cooperate. While you can realistically take an appropriate amount of time to make a decision, no matter how much time you have, it usually doesn't feel like enough. The only cures for the decision-making "blues" are large doses of information and conversation and, when necessary, even larger doses of perspiration—if you have to say no to offers in hand in order to continue the search. After a great deal of analysis and discussions with the very helpful recruiter and the director of her school's career services facility, Jordan accepted the sales management offer. She felt that she wanted to give the business world a chance and that options within other areas could most easily be revived if she wanted to do so in the future. Although this meant she would be assigned an unknown territory after completion of training, that she had the challenges of a sales career ahead, and that she would most likely have to move geographically in order to move up the career path, Jordan felt that this was the right opportunity for now.

By following up the way she did with an employer who had rejected her, by taking dynamic actions, Jordan was able to demonstrate some of her greatest liberal arts abilities—flexibility, communications skills, and adaptability—and she was able to project the positive and tenacious attitudes that were perceived as essential for success on the job. Jordan was truly liberal arts powerful and successful!

Joseph E. Byrne

This anthropology major takes his job search beyond graduation to discover a law-related job.

While the resume was a first step and Joe decided he wanted to remain in New Orleans after graduation, he had quite a distance to go before reaching his goal. With job search and geographic goals in mind in the spring of his senior year, Joe felt confident that something would arise before graduation. As illustrated in the cover letters appearing on pages 134–136, he did a great deal right—developing relationships with the director of his school's career services office, contacting alumni, seeking referrals from all contacts, and identifying sources of posted opportunities. In a job search, however, right doesn't always equate with brief. A job search typically can take three to six months and in many cases it can take six to nine months. So, as discussed before and as Joe learned through experience, one of the first things a soon-to-be-graduated job seeker should do is prepare for the realistic options associated with not having an offer by graduation. Although he had clearly defined functional and geographic goals, Joe's experiences included the typical ups and downs of the job search.

No matter how goal directed or how powerful the job search paperwork, each job seeker must become comfortable with the face-to-face interactions of the job search. Joe was at first a bit uncomfortable with these meetings because he felt awkward explaining his seemingly newfound interest in law. While the best advice he could follow was "read your own resume and believe in it," words spoken often by the director of his school's career services office, Joe still needed to learn by experience. Each new meeting, whether an informational or employment interview, made Joe feel more confident, yet, in time, more frustrated. As he became better at interviewing and interacting with people within his job search network—as graduation grew closer—Joe became frustrated that he wasn't getting any offers. He was getting close, and he was developing relationships with a great many people who offered good advice and the hope that something would arise soon, but he wasn't getting any jobs. With time, Joe began to realize that he was being compared to other soon-to-be college graduates, with law students seeking summer positions, and with experienced legal researchers and paraprofessionals. Joe became increasingly aware that even after taking the liberal arts responsibility for determining and projecting goals and capabilities, he would have to take the liberal arts response-ability to act creatively and maintain a positive outlook.

As he got closer to graduation, Joe began to make contingency plans, for he knew he would have to earn an income if he was to continue his search in New Orleans. Realizing it would be inefficient to move home to New Jersey and direct a long-distance search in New Orleans, Joe used his retail background to obtain a part-time position at a local department store. This would buy him the time he needed, and, although graduation day came and went, Joe felt psychologically and financially confident that he would soon be successful.

The part-time, postgraduation retailing position proved ideal in many ways. Retailing has unusual hours, including evenings and weekends. By structuring his hours appropriately, Joe allowed himself two full working days for his job search efforts. He was able to write letters, make calls, conduct interviews, and use career services resources during this time. In addition to the services offered by his undergraduate college, Joe, as a result of some very well written notes and some alumni support, was offered informal access to services offered by the law school. He was also able to sign up for some courses in business law and legal research at a local community college specializing in paraprofessional training. Not only did this increase his marketable skills, but it made him feel as if he were accomplishing something very goal directed, and it granted him access to additional resources. Of course, Joe updated his resume to cite these new experiences as they arose. The community college had a career services office and a listing of employers who sought graduates of its paralegal program, and it also provided Joe information about search firms that specialized in the legal field. As time went on, as he became a better and better job seeker, and as his resources grew, he got closer and closer to his ultimate goal. He even turned down a part-time position with a law firm because he decided the systems and structures that he had in place offered more than the law-related temporary position.

As the summer went on and as he proved to himself as well as many others that he had the ability to juggle more than one job, Joe received four offers from very prestigious law firms in New Orleans. These offers found their origins in some traditional and some not-so-traditional sources. One, with Daley, Daley, and Rogers, came as a result of continued follow-up of a rejection he had received back in April (see letter on page 136). Another came from a letter-writing campaign Joe implemented early in August when he wrote to all summer employers of Tulane Law School students (from a listing he received from the law school placement office). The remaining two came from referrals made by members of his ever-growing network of contacts. Joe took the job that offered what he believed would be the broadest exposure to different types of litigation and clients. Of course, before doing so, he discussed the pros and cons with the people in his network who he felt would offer the best advice and (semilegal) counsel.

One of the last things he did before he left his retail position was purchase (with an employee discount) several suits for his new job. One of the first things he did after starting his new position was to communicate by letter and phone with all the people he had contacted throughout his job search, thanking them for help, informing them of his new situation, and offering his assistance if it was ever needed. Included in his "closure" activities, Joe met with the director of his undergraduate career services office, offered assistance to any students who might need it in the future, and gave the facility copies of materials and listings that could help others. Joe displayed the abilities, attitudes, and actions to successfully find himself a job, and, whether he realized it or not, laid the groundwork for future searches and professional relationships. He also wanted to help others to be liberal arts powerful—another responsibility and response-ability for liberal arts job seekers.

Rebecca B. Churchill

This music major's job search performance is noteworthy, going beyond a first postgraduation job to an opportunity that matches her talents and goals.

Like many college job seekers, Rebecca sought to undertake a dual-city job search. While she liked Roanoke and had made a great many friends and useful business contacts in this area, she also wanted to look for positions near home in Houston. Although at first Rebecca found that a two-city search required at least four times the effort of a single-city search, as time passed, it seemed that many of her efforts paralleled.

Rebecca began by contacting people with whom she had first communicated during her fund-raising efforts for the Ronald McDonald House. While she felt a bit awkward seeking what she felt was personal and somewhat selfish job search assistance from those who had helped with a very altruistic and selfless community cause, Rebecca wrote letters and made calls to a number of individuals. To her surprise, she found that most were very positive and offered a great deal of information and, in some cases, employment consideration for opportunities in Roanoke and, on occasion, Houston. With time the awkwardness faded and

Rebecca became comfortable adding to her network, making new contacts and seeking assistance as the opportunities arose. She applied the same vigor, creativity, and initiative to her job search networking efforts as she did to the fund-raising ones, while always being sensitive to key differences between the two and extremely diplomatic in her dealings.

Several corporate contacts (often chief executive officers or managers of community and public relations) referred Rebecca to the heads of their human resources areas or individuals in charge of their training departments. It was from these discussions that consideration for positions and, as important, a greater understanding of human resources and training grew. Everyone seemed to reinforce what Rebecca already knew, that "a desire to work with people and to apply teaching skills to a corporate setting" was not enough to obtain a human resources or training position. While they were impressed with Rebecca's background and found her resume to be a true reflection of basic experiences that would qualify her for positions in human resource management and training, most told her of how difficult it was to break in and how traditionally someone with a number of years of "line experience" (experience in actual "line" functions—the business of a given organization—whether sales, manufacturing, etc.) would move into these posts. Rebecca remained undaunted and realistic about her chances for success and continued her job search with a positive attitude, a receptivity to new ideas and approaches, and an ability to incorporate what she was learning along the way. With the help of one of her contacts she created an annotated collection of training materials she had used for the fund-raising campaign. By adding first-person explanations regarding these materials and how they were used, Rebecca illustrated her understanding of relevant concepts and terminology. Thus, she wasn't just a person seeking a first opportunity to learn—she was someone who was knowledgeable seeking an opportunity to implement her knowledge and use her talents. Rebecca contacted the temporary agency where she had worked over a summer to undertake a similar networking effort. While her supervisor had left the organization, the manager of the office, someone Rebecca hardly knew, was so impressed with the way she initiated her communications and made her request for assistance that he soon became a very strong ally and resource for Houston-area opportunities.

As the weeks and months passed, Rebecca began to focus her job search on a manageable number of fields and organizations within these fields, including retailing, insurance, government, and social service.

From experience Rebecca knew that retail firms use professionals for sales associate, management, and executive-level training functions. She learned about the different styles, structures, and approaches used by department stores and specialty stores. Several promising leads arose in this area, and Rebecca was confident that an offer would come with time and, of course, continued communications.

As with retailing, insurance is a sales- and service-dependent field. Insurance organizations must train people for sales, underwriting, claims, and other areas. While people with backgrounds in these functions are often perceived as stronger candidates, Rebecca found insurance firms very receptive to her. As she explored this field, she also became more knowledgeable about another area of human resources—compensation and benefits. This was knowledge that would pay off in time.

Federal, state, and local government agencies, because of the complex structures within which they exist, require professionals to train personnel to work within the agencies and with those who use the agencies' services. While Rebecca was interested, she also experienced the frustration associated with seeking a job in these areas. Although it wasn't easy, Rebecca filled out appropriate forms, followed procedures, and, as suggested by several people in her network, continued to be assertive in her requests for informational and employment interviews. She determined it was worth the effort because some of the more interesting positions involved training those who provide services to children and adults with health-related disabilities.

Social service organizations not affiliated with government entities have paid professional staffs that include training professionals. These people often train trainers and volunteers. Rebecca was, because of her fund-raising experience, very comfortable with this model and was a strong candidate for positions with organizations like the United Way, Girl Scouts, Campfire Girls, Red Cross, and American Heart Association. In truth, Rebecca judged this area as the one where she would most like a position.

As a result of referrals, Rebecca also communicated with consulting firms having human resources management and training areas. These firms provided training services for client organizations (some of which were organizations Rebecca was communicating with directly). Many had specialized areas of expertise such as sales, and some, although a small number, even specialized in fund-raising.

Graduation grew nearer, but Rebecca tried to control her anxiety. Because she realized that an early graduation date (December) would most likely mean that her job search would not be completed, Rebecca planned to move back to Houston and make several trips to Roanoke for her job search and her fund-raising efforts for the Ronald McDonald House. Well, graduation came and went and Rebecca carried on assertively and effectively.

Early in the spring, Rebecca received an offer to join the Houston-based staff of a consulting firm that specialized in creating benefits programs for large corporations. Although the position was not titled "trainer," but "client services representative," it required training and presentation skills. Basically, Rebecca would be teaching employees of client organizations about new benefits packages (including health care, retirement, and other programs) and how to complete claim forms for these services. She would be called upon first to teach all current employees about the new plan and later to conduct new-employee orientation programs and answer any questions as they might arise. While cocktail party advice might include "do not accept the first offer you receive," Rebecca knew better than to take this particular axiom at face value. She determined that this opportunity was right—at least for her immediate future. Rebecca accepted the offer, but she kept her network intact and active by writing thank-you notes and timely follow-up letters detailing how she was doing, what she was learning, and what her future goals entailed. About ten months after starting her first postgraduation job, Rebecca received two other offers of employment. One was with a retail firm as a trainer and the other was with the United Way to enter a structured intern program that involved experiences in agency management and fund-raising. While the second option required a cut in pay, involved a move from Houston, and did not guarantee a specific situation after completion of the yearlong program, Rebecca determined that this would be an ideal use of her talents and that she would be happiest in the long term if she entered the social and community services field.

Rebecca's liberal arts power did not wane after she accepted her first job. The *abilities* and *attitudes* she possessed and the *actions* she took became a process that she learned could be turned up or down at her discretion. She became more powerful, revived the process when desired, and obtained additional offers. While it is obvious that liberal arts resumes become more powerful as additional employment experiences are added, it may not be as clear that liberal arts job seekers can become more and more powerful at job search if they perceive their efforts as ongoing rather than one time only.

Kathy Fish

This government major's on-campus recruiting pays off with many offers and, ultimately, a job with the fed.

Developing a liberal arts powerful resume made Kathy more confident. The assessment and goal setting that were a part of this process became the cornerstones of a relatively short but highly successful job search. More important, by going to her school's career services office, Kathy began to develop a strong relationship with this facility and its professionals. Although this is not the case for most liberal arts job seekers, the resources offered there proved to be all Kathy needed to obtain job offers.

Kathy's school had a very extensive on-campus recruiting program in which a large number of organizations, including banks and government agencies, came to interview students for entry-level opportunities. There were also several consortium interview programs in which the students of several schools meet with recruiters in cities such as Boston, New York, Chicago, and Washington, D.C. After her initial visit for resume help, Kathy attended almost every workshop, seminar, and company information session that was offered. She felt less anxious and more in control of the job search process as she learned about and participated in the numerous offerings of this facility. Kathy took her efforts seriously, fitting these activities into her busy academic and extracurricular schedule. She summed up her approach by stating that she was treating her job search as if it were a required course.

Kathy became very adept at scheduling on-campus interviews. By understanding the rules and procedures of her school's recruiting program she was able to sign up for the ones she wanted and often filled in when other students canceled. She used the multipurpose resume for most of her early interviews but developed a banking-related one later in the recruiting season. Kathy's involvement in the on-campus recruiting program resulted in her receiving a number of callbacks, and she was invited to visit the offices of recruiting organizations and undergo additional interviews. At the urging of her career counselor, however, Kathy maintained a realistic attitude about this process and didn't let her expectations get too high. While on-campus recruiting was convenient, Kathy also did not want to limit her search to recruiters who participated in this program.

As on-campus recruiting ended and as her callbacks continued, Kathy became involved in two of her school's off-campus programs. She had interviews in Boston and Washington during her spring break. As anticipated, Kathy did quite well with her banking interviews, and she was particularly pleased with the number of interviews she had with Washington-based agencies. While in Boston and Washington, Kathy interviewed with the Federal Reserve for entry-level opportunities. Of all the organizations she had interviewed with, this one seemed to best combine her interest in banking and government. When she returned to school she asked for advice from her career counselor concerning how best to communicate with the organization without appearing overly aggressive. Guided by her counselor, Kathy completed additional research on the opportunities offered by the Federal Reserve, wrote a few letters, made some calls, and asked a professor to call in support of her candidacy.

Kathy also communicated with the financial aid and residence life offices of her school concerning her interest in obtaining postgraduation employment, and she touched base with the people she worked with on the Maine Senate campaign. These discussions were positive, but Kathy soon realized that the more structured recruiting interviews would result in offers and demand decisions well before any serious consideration would be granted by these potential employers. After discussing this and related concerns with her career counselor, she decided to focus most of her attention on recruiting; she would follow up and explore these other options only if necessary.

Kathy's dedicated approach to using the resources of her career planning and placement office, specifically the recruiting activities, paid off early in the spring. She received several offers from banks for operations positions, from retail firms for executive training programs, and, most important, from the Federal Reserve for a training program that would expose her to the workings of this agency, prepare her for an entry-level, audit-related post, and place her on a career path that would offer challenges in a variety of areas. Because she had done extensive research early and because she had completed so many interviews, she was able to compare and contrast organizations and opportunities. Kathy found that her decision was not too difficult to make. She accepted the offer from the Washington office of the Federal Reserve and looked forward to the opportunity to combine her interests in banking and government.

Cathy Lynne Giles

Geographic flexibility yields high returns for an economics major banking on success in a targeted field.

Although she was very directed and very experienced, Cathy's job search was not as easy as she had anticipated. While she was able to focus her liberal arts power through clearly defined goals and could easily document skills and capabilities as well as control the means by which she projected these through her resume, Cathy was unable to control some critical variables. The regions in which Cathy wanted to direct her search, the Southeast and Southwest, were going through tough economic times, and, most significant, the banking and savings and loan industries were bearing the brunt of the downturn. Cathy's abilities were without question and her attitude was confident and upbeat, but no matter how effective her actions, they could not change the fact that potential employers were not receptive to her candidacy. They were impressed with her background and apologetic in their rejections. They asked Cathy to be patient, but they told her that they were having difficulty retaining employees and were not interested in hiring new ones no matter how qualified they were.

Cathy soon determined that her functional goal was more important than her geographic goals—she redirected her search to larger organizations in the Northeast, specifically New York and Boston. While there were several aspects of the New York life-style that Cathy did not look forward to, she realistically concluded that it was best to go where the opportunities were and meet any difficulties as they arose. Cathy used her references as well as resources available through her school's career services office to develop a hit list of potential employers. She arranged trips to these cities over the winter and spring breaks, planning to combine family visits with interviews, and informed all she corresponded with that she would be available to meet (at her own expense) during these periods. Few recruiters could resist meeting such an interesting and inexpensive recruit.

Cathy's visits to Boston and New York were hectic and fruitful. She met with recruiters from most of the large commercial banks to discuss lending opportunities and, quite by accident, became aware of and interviewed for investment banking positions. Because Cathy had been so focused on commercial loan posts and because recruiting for investment banking options was often limited to schools in the Northeast, she knew very little about these opportunities. These positions involve application of research and analytical skills to the researching and structuring of deals. While financial analysts conduct research similar to the risk analysis done by commercial lending officers, they do not apply sales and relationship development talents as often to their day-to-day responsibilities.

Because Cathy wanted to use her banking and sales experiences, she accepted one of the three offers she received to enter commercial-lending-oriented training programs and rejected two investment banking offers. She was able to find a compromise to her life-style concerns by taking a job with a Boston-based organization that did a great deal of business in the Southwest. Cathy was told that her background and preferences would be considered when assignments were made and that it was possible that within twelve to eighteen months she could be working in an office in Texas.

At first glance, by virtue of qualifications presented on a resume, you would have expected Cathy Giles to have little difficulty obtaining the position stated in her Career Goal. Well, no matter how powerful the resume, no matter how strong your abilities nor how determined your attitude, actions are the essential elements of a successful job search. In this case, actions did speak louder than words, for Cathy was able to adapt to circumstances beyond her control, redirect her energies, and persevere to reach her goal. She did what her liberal arts education trained her to do: assess situations, identify alternatives, act resourcefully, and succeed.

Lawrence Herder

Forced to change, working at his job search as a full-time job, a mid-life career changer finds a new beginning.

Although Lawrence's job search should not be called "typical," for no job search, especially one conducted by a person with over twenty-five years of experience, is typical, in following the advice of his career counselor as well as his own sales-heightened instincts, he did follow some identifiable patterns.

No matter how confident and psychologically strong the individual, when confronted by a job search brought on by circumstances "not of one's own choosing," feelings of anger, self-doubt, and, yes, loss, arise. Lawrence was fortunate because the firm that let him go offered a severance package that included outplacement counseling and six months of salary and benefits. During their very first session, Lawrence's counselor outlined the services he could offer (as well as those he could not), discussed the psychological aspects of the situation, and suggested some short-term-action and long-term-action steps.

Lawrence wisely decided to take no job search action for a while. He and his wife took a relatively inexpensive, but very relaxing, ten-day "decompression vacation." It was during this time that Lawrence was able to let go of his strongest negative thoughts and emotions and direct his energies toward developing a positive attitude.

Upon his return, Lawrence began a thorough analysis of his employment history and documented his past experiences by means of some very structured exercises given him by his counselor. After several weeks of introspection and research, he established job search targets. As noted earlier, Lawrence decided to look for a job in advertising sales. Once this was done Lawrence was able to create a targeted resume and appropriate job strategies. He also created a financial plan that paralleled the time span that he believed would be necessary to obtain a job within his field of choice. He and his wife identified income sources, including severance pay, unemployment insurance, and investment returns, as well as expenses and budgeted accordingly. This, he hoped, would alleviate some of the financial and psychological pressures that might arise during the three-to-nine-month period of the job search.

Also at the suggestion of his counselor, Lawrence developed a weekly routine that would get him out of the house and into a professional environment. For at least three days a week, he would spend the time that he wasn't involved in employment or informational interviews at the outplacement firm's offices. They provided him with a telephone, numerous resource materials, access to counselors as needed, and the clerical support required to complete all of his job search correspondence. Lawrence worked at *his* job search as if it were a job. He was diligent in his efforts and, whenever possible, helped others who had been let go by Offices Midwest. As a result of his research efforts Lawrence found that he felt very comfortable in the library of his alma mater. He spent a great deal of his additional time there, using the publications and professionals (reference librarians) available to him. Lawrence also became more involved in a professional association of which he had been a member for a number of years. He attended monthly meetings and seminars that dealt with issues of interest. Lawrence, although unemployed, had a routine that required that a great deal of time and attention be paid to job search–related activities.

Basically, Lawrence's job search involved networking with existing contacts and developing new ones, identifying and communicating with organizations related to his goals, using search firms, and responding to posted opportunities. Lawrence contacted many of his business associates, informed them of his situation, shared his goals, and asked their assistance. He was able to convey a very positive attitude and projected a very professional demeanor. Thus, he diffused any awkwardness that might be felt by someone who didn't know how to interact with a person who was out of work.

Lawrence believed that the people who worked for his previous firm's advertising agency would be his most important contacts, for their media planners had relationships with media salespeople. This proved to be correct. Using resources available through the outplacement firm and the college library, Lawrence developed a hit list of television and radio stations, advertising sales groups, and other media-related employers. Rather than conduct a mass-mail campaign, Lawrence developed and implemented a direct-sales approach to identifying the needs of these organizations, communicating with senior managers, and presenting what he could do to meet critical needs. Thus, he used his job search as a means of showing the talents he would use on the job.

As appropriate for someone with a great deal of experience, Lawrence also communicated with and used the services of several search firms. Because he had used these firms when seeking new employees over the years, Lawrence had developed relationships with quite a few search professionals and had intimate knowledge of their approaches. He knew that they would not actually "search for" nor find him a job, but they were good sources of opportunities that would not be posted elsewhere and they could enhance his networking efforts. Also, larger national firms could expand Lawrence's search beyond geographic boundaries by means of databases and personal referrals. He was goal directed in his communications with these organizations and made sure to follow up on these contacts as closely as he did with potential employers.

While he didn't expect much from this approach, Lawrence regularly checked and responded to employment advertisements in regional and national newspapers and the postings that appeared in professional association newsletters.

For Lawrence, as for most job seekers, it was a matter of persistence and patience, maintaining the proper attitude, and taking effective action long enough to uncover the right opportunities. But for experienced job seekers it is often more difficult the longer the search takes. The anger and self-doubt can recur, and the financial pressures increase as time goes on. With the support of his wife, his counselor, and his friends and with the ability to implement a well-thought-out set of strategies, Lawrence's search ended after a bit more than four months of effort. While several discussions with potential employers resulted in serious consideration and Lawrence came extremely close to accepting offers and negotiating some situations until they reached the offer stage, he waited for what he believed would be the right situation.

By networking with ad agency contacts, Lawrence uncovered an opening for a Director of Sales and Marketing for a small and growing magazine and book publishing group. His sales and marketing management background and, specifically, his experience training and overseeing a sales force were exactly what this firm was looking for. Lawrence felt as if this organization offered him a chance to try something new, to enter media-related sales, while in return he offered them some*thing* (not some*one*) old, his proven abilities. He welcomed this opportunity to use his talents in a new and exciting area. Although circumstances beyond his control had forced Lawrence to seek this situation, by taking a powerful approach to his job search he gained control over the situation, waited until he wanted to say yes, and felt very confident that his future would include exciting new challenges and rewards.

Robert D. Jay

Retailing was not right, but, for this psychology major, accounting added up to the right choice.

Robert's goal made the early stages of his job search relatively easy, for it was easy to identify retail firms, interview with them through on-campus recruiting, and contact them directly. While gaining interviews wasn't a problem and Robert seemed to do quite well, a problem did arise. Robert's reactions to the initial and callback interviews wasn't what he expected. His interest in retailing, while based on thorough research and a great many informational interviews, seemed to wane as he went through the interview process. He wasn't getting more excited about the prospects of an offer, but less. Robert discussed this with some of the alumni with whom he had interviewed during his research phase. They suggested that he complete all of the retail interviews and obtain as many offers in this area as possible but that he also broaden his search to other fields. Robert's decision to develop a multipurpose resume proved to be a good one as his job search efforts expanded to include more than retail firms.

Robert revived his research and goal-setting activities, reading about other fields, talking to more people about their jobs, and attending company information sessions. During this time, an accounting professor passed on some materials he had received regarding a graduate program in accounting at New York University that combined school with employment in an accounting firm. Robert hadn't really considered going directly on to graduate school. He felt it would be best to work for a while and then decide whether additional schooling would be good for his personal or career growth. Coincidentally, or maybe not, Robert soon received an invitation to attend an information session given by an accounting firm that participated in this program. It seemed that the firm had asked for recommendations from professors and Robert was referred by several. Robert found the presentation regarding the program and the opportunities offered by the firm interesting. As of that evening he added the NYU Master of Accounting program to his newly developing list of options. He was now focusing his attention on fields that would use his quantitative and problem-solving skills as well as his people skills.

Robert interviewed with five of the eight firms that sponsored students for the NYU program and a number of other organizations, including computer consulting firms and commercial banks. The more interviews he had with accounting firms and the more he learned about the NYU program (he met several program alumni during callback interviews), the more he wanted to receive an offer and be admitted into the program. Robert got his wish. He was admitted into the program and got offers from three of the sponsoring firms he interviewed with, as well as offers from some retailers and banks. Robert decided that retail wasn't really right, for now, so he accepted the offer from the accounting firm that he felt matched his personality, and he entered the NYU program a few weeks after graduation.

Writing Your Resume

Now that you have taken stock of your skills, reviewed the sample resumes, and focused in on three or four job targets, you are prepared to actually write your resume. There are of course many ways to write a resume, and there are many topics that can be included in one. You will have to decide which topics are appropriate for *your* resume in accordance with your objectives, your background, and other factors. The order in which topics appear on a resume is also variable. By ordering material in a particular way, you highlight the information that you judge to be of most importance.

The sample resumes that appear in this book illustrate many ways to organize a resume. To help you decide which topics are appropriate for your resume, a brief discussion of possible topics follows.

The Contents

Identifying Information

Your name, address, and telephone number should be placed in a prominent position, usually at the top of the resume. Some students give a permanent address and a school address if both will be used during the job search. If your address or phone number changes while you are looking for a job, it is important that you correct and reprint your resume and send follow-up letters announcing the change to those people you have already contacted.

Objective

You may include a statement describing your career goal, job target, or reason for using the resume. This is not appropriate for all resumes or all job seekers. One of the most important decisions you must make concerning the content of your resume is whether or not to include a statement of this type.

Stating your Objective tells potential employers that you are headed in a certain direction, informs them of your reasons for making contact, and serves as a focal point from which they can review and analyze the remainder of the resume. The Objective does not necessarily limit you or prevent the potential employer from considering you for positions other than those stated, but it does indicate that you have preferences. Some employers will not consider you for positions other than those specified in your statement of goals, but through follow-up contacts you can encourage them to do so.

Those job seekers who possess clear goals will want to present

One of the most important decisions you must make at the outset is whether or not to include a statement describing your career goal.

them on their resume. Those who are considering more than one professional goal may develop more than one resume, each presenting a different Objective. Job seekers who are unsure of their career goals may develop a resume without a statement of Objective. But they can, and must, communicate a sense of direction in other ways. Cover letters and documents such as a Summary of Qualifications, which are distributed along with the resume (and which are illustrated and discussed later in this book), can serve this purpose.

Do not be afraid to state an Objective. Doing so does not mean making a lifelong commitment to a particular job or field. And a well-written Objective can be very useful in communicating goals and qualifications. It can focus and, thus, increase the liberal arts power projected by your resume. As sunlight can be focused by a magnifying glass to set fire to a piece of paper, so can an Objective ignite a resume. If you do use one, make sure that it tells potential employers clearly what you want to do, using job titles and functional descriptions that are recognizable and that reflect your knowledge of the areas in which you are seeking employment. A vaguely worded Objective can do more harm than good.

Remember that a vaguely worded Objective can do more harm than good.

Activities and exercises outlined in the section called Steps to Writing Your Resume are designed to help you define your career goals.

Education

Include undergraduate and graduate study, as well as foreign study and special academic programs. Degrees, institutions and their locations, dates graduated or dates attended, and majors and minors can be included. As with all entries on a resume, you decide what to include. Academic course work and areas of academic emphasis, if they are related to your objective, may be included. Scholarships, honor society memberships, special awards, and grade point averages can also be mentioned. You may wish to give your GPA in your major or some other specific academic area in addition to or instead of your cumulative GPA. Some students give their averages for a certain period of time, such as their junior and senior years, if this information is more flattering. Education can be presented under special headings, such as Science Education, Computer Education, or Business-related Education, which allows the job seeker to group related experiences and give his or her resume a particular focus.

Experience

Include specific accomplishments, emphasize skills, and use action verbs when describing your experiences.

List full-time and part-time jobs, as well as volunteer work, internships, externships, and other career-related experiences. State the titles you held and the names of the organizations and describe the experiences in active, skills-oriented terms. Whenever possible, mention specific accomplishments. A common way of presenting this information is in reverse chronological order. You can also group related experiences together under special titles, such as Counseling Experience, Computer Experience, or Business Experience.

Extracurricular and Community Activities

Give the names of the organizations and, if appropriate, offices held, accomplishments, and special projects. Your description of your activities should make potential employers aware of the skills you have acquired.

If your activities associated with a club, school group, or community organization are directly related to the career or job you want, you may describe them under an Experience heading instead of under Activities. Whether you received payment for your contributions of time and energy should not determine where you describe it on your resume. The nature of your responsibilities and their relationship to your career goals should be the deciding factors.

Commenting on the importance of extracurricular activities from the perspective of one who hires many college graduates, a district manager of one of America's leading companies says: "We look for people who set goals for themselves and then set specific plans to reach those goals. We have found that students who have been actively involved in a number of activities while in college have already dealt with the problem solving and priority setting which are important in our field."

Special Categories

Almost anything can be treated as a special category on a resume. Presenting information under its own heading is a good way of highlighting it. The categories outlined below—Skills, Qualifications, Languages, and Computer Languages—are the most common.

Other special headings might include Supervisory Experience, Finance Background, Teaching Activities, and Travel and International Experience. You can use such special categories to support your Objective and to project a sense of direction to employers. The Objective focuses the attention of the potential employer on a particular job, while the information you give in special categories documents and explains the qualifications you have for that job.

• *Skills*

List and discuss the skills you possess that can be used on the job. Document your skills with examples of work, activities, and educational experiences. Functional resumes, which are discussed later, make particularly prominent use of skills headings, but other types of resumes can have them too.

• *Qualifications*

You can use a Qualifications section to summarize your skills, education, character, and motivation in a way that shows how they qualify you for the employment you seek.

• *Languages*

List foreign languages you know and briefly describe your level of fluency in each.

• *Computer Languages*

Be sure to list any computer languages you know and indicate your level of expertise in each of them. This information can be included with a summary of college course work or highlighted under a separate heading.

Interests

It is appropriate to include a few informal statements about your travel experiences, hobbies, and interests, but do this only if you have extra space to fill.

If you wish, you may include a few informal statements about your travel experiences, hobbies, and interests in order to tell prospective employers a bit about the "nonbusiness" aspects of your background. It is best to leave this information off the resume if you need space for more important information. If you have acquired special skills as a result of pursuing your interests, discuss these skills under a special heading, rather than under Interests, to ensure that employers will read this information.

Personal Data

Personal data, such as height, weight, date and place of birth, and marital status were formerly standard items on a resume. Now they are usually omitted. Equal employment opportunity regulations require that employers recruit and hire in a nondiscriminatory manner, without regard to race, handicap, religion, color, sex, age, or national origin, and such information is now considered to have no bearing on a person's ability to do a job. Some job seekers combine interests and personal data under the headings Personal or Background Information and include such items as hobbies, travel, or unusual childhood experiences. But, unless you believe this information truly enhances your qualifications or you need to fill up the page, these topics are probably best left off your resume.

References and Recommendations

Whether you ask people to write letters of recommendation or simply to serve as references, you should be sure to keep them informed of your job search activities.

The names of references can be given along with their professional titles, addresses, and phone numbers if those involved have given you permission to use this information. If you have letters on file at your college or university, you may state on the resume, "Placement dossier, including letters of recommendation, available from _____," giving the name of the appropriate university office. "References available upon request" may also be added to the end of the resume, but since employers will request them if they are needed, the phrase may be superfluous and can be omitted.

To save space on your resume and, perhaps more important, to give yourself greater flexibility and greater control over your references, you can develop and distribute several different lists of references, printed on separate sheets. You can create individualized lists for different job targets, and you can change the references as you meet more people who can assist you.

You should be aware that there is a difference between references and recommendations. References are people who can tell potential employers about your background and how you might perform on the job. These individuals may be past employers, teachers, and others who have known you in academic settings, as well as people who know you in a personal context. Recommendations, better stated as letters of recommendation, are written documents that tell potential employers about your background and capabilities.

Always remember to use references assertively and effectively. They should be active participants in your job search.

Always remember to be prepared to use references assertively and effectively. They should be active participants in your job search, not just passive names on a piece of paper. The first five letters of the word "reference" spell "refer," and you should feel comfortable asking those you use as references to refer you to potential employers or helpful job search resources. Keep them informed of how things are going, solicit their reactions and advice concerning situations, and don't be afraid to ask them to contact employers directly, even if their opinions have not yet been solicited. A surprise testimonial from one of your references to a potential employer can be powerful.

Under the Family Educational Rights and Privacy Act of 1974—referred to by some as "the Buckley Amendment" because James Buckley, a senator from New York, authored portions of the legislation—students are entitled to read letters of recommendation in their placement files unless they waive their right of access. The issue of whether you should waive your right of access, creating a completely "confidential" recommendation, is one that has been debated since the creation of the law in 1974. I do not believe that this is an issue the student job seeker should be concerned with. It should not matter to an employer whether you have read your letters of recommendation or not. What should matter is whether you have the qualifications to perform the tasks associated with the job you are applying for. Most employers rely much more on their own judgments of your qualifications than on the judgments of persons who have written recommendations. You should not be asking anyone to write a recommendation if there is a possibility they might write something that questions your capabilities. If you prepare your references by providing them a copy of your resume and by sharing with them your goals and your own analysis of your qualifications for particular types of jobs, you should have nothing to worry about.

Most employers rely much more on their own judgments of your qualifications than on the judgments of persons who have written recommendations.

In addition, you should always request copies of letters of recommendation. If you receive copies, you can then waive your right of access and still know what appears in your file or you can maintain your right of access, depending on your personal opinions concerning this issue. If someone refuses to provide you with a copy, you should explore the reasons why and perhaps withdraw your request for a letter of recommendation or maintain your right of access to that particular letter.

Resume Formats

There are three basic resume formats—chronological, functional, and combination.

Chronological

The chronological resume presents information in reverse chronological order under major headings such as the traditional ones discussed above. This is the most common type of resume and the easiest to develop because it simply lists experiences in the reverse order in which they happened.

Functional

The functional resume presents information under skills headings such as those mentioned in the discussion of "Special Categories" above. Abilities and experiences are grouped according to job-related functions, such as research, statistical analysis, or supervision. This kind of resume can be more work to write, but it can also be very effective for liberal arts job seekers who want to highlight skills that can be transferred from one field of endeavor to another. This format can be used successfully by recent graduates as well as by those reentering the job market or changing career fields.

Combination

The combination resume represents a mix of the chronological and functional approaches, presenting some information under traditional headings and organizing other elements according to job functions.

By including skills headings on your resume, you present potential employers with the conclusions you want them to reach.

All three formats can be used effectively by liberal arts job seekers. I would like to emphasize, however, that for most people it is a good idea to incorporate some type of functional component in the resume. Liberal arts job seekers who think and speak in terms of skills usually have the most success. Unless you have a great deal of experience directly related to the job you want (in which case your work experience will speak for itself), you should either use skills headings or include a Summary of Skills or Qualifications section. By doing so, you present potential employers with the conclusions you want them to reach. This is better than leaving the interpretation of your abilities to chance.

As stated by another human resources professional: "After reading traditional chronological resumes, I often find myself asking, 'What skills does this person possess?' Many times students have done a great deal—in the classroom, at work, and elsewhere—and have developed some very marketable skills through these experiences. However, if they do not list their skills for me, they leave it up to me to identify them. What if I miss their most important skills in the interview or in a quick reading of the resume?"

You may, of course, decide against a functional resume or even against a combination resume. After examining some of the sample resumes, beginning on page 45, you may decide that a chronological approach is best for you. If you do not incorporate a functional component in your resume, however, you should at least prepare a functional worksheet for yourself to help you assess your skills and prepare for interviews.

Remember that whatever format you choose, your resume must be organized so that potential employers can locate information quickly. If you create a functional resume, make sure it is well organized and has in some way identified your job titles and the organizations you have worked for, as well as your extracurricular activities and the organizations you have belonged to, and that the skills headings are appropriate to the jobs you are seeking. If you create a chronological resume, be selective in the items you include so that they too are appropriate for your goals. If you create a combination resume, make sure the functional section presents your qualifications in the most dynamic way possible and illustrates your ability to analyze your greatest strengths.

Whatever the approach, your resume must project your liberal arts power and your on-the-job performance power. Your resume is a reflection of your ability to perform a critical task. It will in most cases be the first thing about you that is judged by a potential employer. This document, as well as all communications (verbal and written) and actions, must reflect job-related abilities and attitudes in order to be powerful and effective.

Targeted Resumes vs. Multipurpose Resumes

After you have decided which of the three basic formats to use, you should then think about whether your needs would be best served by a targeted resume or a multipurpose resume. Targeted resumes contain a statement of the job seeker's objective and present information in a way that supports that objective. Multipurpose resumes, on the other hand, include no specific statement of objective, and they can therefore be presented to potential employers in a number of different fields.

It is best to limit yourself to three major job targets and, at most, three different resumes.

I suggest that you develop a targeted resume, if at all possible. As discussed earlier, resumes with statements of Objective and supporting functional sections focus liberal arts power and, therefore, can be very effective. If you have not decided on a single Objective, you can develop more than one resume, or you can develop a very well written multipurpose resume. If you choose to write a multipurpose resume, you must be sure to explain your goals and qualifications in the cover letters you write to potential employers. Some of the analyses in this book explain how you can add documents such as a Summary of Qualifications or a Skills Summary to a multipurpose resume in order to orient it toward a particular kind of job. You may wish to develop one multipurpose resume and several supplementary pages, one for each Objective.

I believe it is wise, however, to limit yourself to three resumes or, if you decide on a multipurpose resume, three supplementary pages. You should be able to limit yourself to three major job targets. In fact, more than this at a given time is too much for most job seekers to handle. You do not want to suffer the embarrassment of sending the wrong resume to an employer; also keep in mind that the cost of developing a good-looking resume can be substantial.

Length

If your resume is longer than one page, make sure that the first page contains the most important information.

I do not accept the myth of the one-page resume. Your resume should be as concise as possible, but it must communicate essential information. Do not limit yourself to an arbitrary length of one page before you have written it. If you have honed it down and edited out unnecessary information, and it is still longer than one page—fine! Employers read information that is organized and well presented. If your resume turns out to be longer than a page, just make sure that the first page contains the most important information. Make the employer want to read the second page.

Writing Your Rough Draft

The first thing you have to do before you begin to write is decide whether you will be developing a targeted resume or a multipurpose resume. If you have chosen to write a targeted resume, first write down your job Objective, referring to your Job Target Chart and your list of three first-choice jobs. Even if you opt not to include an employment Objective, your resume must show potential employers that you are familiar with your own capabilities and qualifications. Knowledge of self and knowledge of job functions are the keys to a successful liberal arts job search, and your resume must reflect this knowledge if it is going to work for you.

Next review the discussions of resume contents (page 107) and formats (page 112) and refer to the sample resumes you judged appropriate for your purposes in order to determine which format and headings you will use. Then make a list of the headings you think you will want to include. If you decide to use a chronological format, review your Chronological Flowchart and mark the entries you wish to include on your resume. If you decide to write a functional resume, review your Skills Flowchart to identify which skills you will feature and to decide under which headings they should appear.

You should now be ready to write your first draft. Don't be concerned at all about appearance or length at this point. Continually refer to your flowcharts and your Job Target Chart and base your entries on the items you highlighted as the most important.

Write as freely and as quickly as you can, and refrain from being overly critical at this point. Include everything you think you might want in the final draft. (You will probably be surprised to find that your rough draft ends up being several pages long!) The more comprehensive your rough draft is, the more effective your final draft will be. Use a format you like, but do not worry too much about the placement of headings or about highlighting techniques. Once your first draft is written, you will be able to relax and edit it and think about ways to improve the layout.

State your accomplishments clearly and with conviction. Don't be modest. This is your chance to brag.

When describing academic, extracurricular, and employment experiences, be as thorough and descriptive as possible. Use active, skills-oriented phrasing. Refer to the list of appropriate action words and phrases below for suggestions.

When describing experiences, cite specific accomplishments and don't be modest. This is your chance to brag. If a fraternity or sorority fund-raising drive you chaired raised the most money of all campus organizations, say so. In fact, it's even a good idea to state exactly how much money was raised. If you figured out a way to effectively promote and sell certain items in a store you worked in, include that. State your accomplishments clearly and with conviction. Be proud of what you have done.

Don't feel that you have to use complete sentences in all sections. It's perfectly acceptable to use "telegram style," omitting articles and pronouns, especially first-person pronouns, which do not add to the clarity of descriptions. The phrasing should make sense, but it should also be as succinct as possible.

Action Words and Phrases

accommodated	advised	assisted
achieved	advocated	assumed
acquainted	altered	attached
activated	analyzed	attained
adapted	appraised	augmented
administered	approved	authorized
advertised	assembled	

analyzed procedures to assess their efficiency
analyzed ideas and situations from different perspectives
applied research data to develop proposals or reach conclusions
applied theory and abstract concepts to work settings
applied appropriate resources to problem-solving strategies
assessed needs of organization and implemented improvements

balanced	communicated	controlled
built	conceived	converted
classified	condensed	coordinated
collected	conferred	counseled
combined	consolidated	created
commanded	consulted	curtailed

created innovative solutions to problems
compiled, organized, and analyzed data
conveyed a positive image to the public

demonstrated	developed	discovered
designated	directed	dispatched
designed	disclosed	displayed
determined	discontinued	distributed

delegated responsibility to others for completion of tasks
defined parameters of problem situations
described events or objects accurately
designed experiments or research procedures
demonstrated appropriate assertiveness in various settings and
    circumstances

economized	evaluated	familiarized
educated	examined	formulated
eliminated	exchanged	governed
employed	executed	grouped
encouraged	expanded	guaranteed
established	expedited	guided
estimated	extended	

evaluated information and presented analyses
expressed opinions and preferences without offending others
formulated questions to clarify problems or to assess attitudes
generated trust and confidence of others

illustrated	initiated	inventoried
improved	instructed	invested
increased	interpreted	investigated
informed	introduced	lectured

identified alternative course of action and strategies
identified information for specific situations and needs
identified issues critical to making decisions or solving problems
listened with objectivity and utilized information for problem
    solving

maintained	motivated	prescribed
managed	observed	procured
measured	obtained	produced
merged	operated	publicized
minimized	organized	published
modernized	originated	
modified	planned	

managed time and resources effectively
motivated and managed personnel
marketed self, a product, or a service
organized people and material to achieve goals

recommended	simplified	terminated
rectified	solved	trained
reduced	sponsored	transferred
regulated	stabilized	transformed
removed	strengthened	unified
reorganized	studied	updated
repaired	supervised	utilized
replaced	supplemented	vetoed
reported	surpassed	wrote
restored	taught	

suggested possible long-range and short-range outcomes of actions
wrote effective promotional materials and designed advertising brochures

Critiquing Your Rough Draft

Now that your rough draft is completed, use the Critiquing Guidelines that appear below to judge the quality of the draft, make appropriate changes, and eventually develop the typed draft of your resume.

Friends, family members, and former employers should all be able to tell you if you've left out something significant.

At this stage, you should be more concerned about writing style and graphics. Review the sample resumes to identify phrasing, highlighting techniques, and layouts that suit your purposes. Use a dictionary to find the correct spelling of words that you are not sure of. The next draft should be as close to the final draft in content and format as possible, so this critiquing stage is very important.

Once you've worked through several revisions and *before* you have your resume typeset and duplicated, ask a few people to critique your final version. Friends, family members, and former employers are good choices; they should all be able to tell you if you've left out something significant. Career counselors, placement officers, and other professionals who look at resumes all the time are also bound to have a lot of good, constructive advice.

After you've considered everyone's comments, incorporated some of their suggestions, and decided on your final version, proofread your resume very thoroughly. Then have five of your friends proofread it, and then, before you hand it over to the printer, proof it again. *Your resume must be error free.* If you find that it has a typographical error, a dangling phrase, an incomplete correction, or a stray mark of any kind, retype it, or, if it's already been typeset, have it redone. It's better to invest the extra money to have your resume corrected than to use a resume that presents you as a person who does not pay attention to detail.

Critiquing Guidelines

Review the following questions to judge your resume's quality and effectiveness. You should be able to answer yes to each question. If you cannot do so, examine your rough draft carefully and make changes that will allow you to answer affirmatively. If completing your first critiquing, ignore questions that make reference to a final draft.

APPEARANCE

Is it neat and easy to read?

Do topic headings stand out?

Have you used space to highlight headings and important information?

Have you used underlining, CAPITALIZATION, **bold typing,** *varied type styles,* and spacing to highlight important information?

Were you consistent in placement of headings and content—centered, margined, indented?

Have you used the best type style, or styles, to create the image you want?

Is your resume free of typographical errors, misspelled words, messy erasures?

Does your resume look professional and businesslike?

Is your final draft clear and dark enough for good duplication?

CONTENTS

Identifying information

Does your name stand out?

Are your address and phone number easy to find?

If more than one address or phone number appears, is it clear when each is to be used?

Objective statement

If it appears, does it project knowledge of the desired career field by using appropriate phrasing?

Does it stress job titles, job functions, your skills, or a combination of these?

Have you considered developing a multipurpose resume without an Objective, as well as one or more resumes with Objectives?

Education

Have you presented school(s), degree(s), area(s) of concentration, courses, honors?

If an Objective is stated, have you highlighted academic experiences that are most relevant?

Are grades or grade point averages presented, if complimentary?

Have you presented academic-related information appropriate for your goals?

Experience

Have you included all experiences that project skills and accomplishments?

Did you describe experiences in active phrasing, using skills-oriented and functionally descriptive words?

Did you discuss achievements and accomplishments, noting facts and figures when appropriate?

Are experiences grouped according to topics that are related to your goals or stated Objective?

Have you really thought about all of the activities, paid and volunteer, that contributed to your developing the skills and abilities you possess?

Do job titles, organizations, or both, stand out as well as you desire? Could they be easily found by a potential employer?

Have you presented experiences in reverse chronological order? If not, is there logic behind the presentation?

Have you included dates with your descriptions? If not, do you have a good reason for leaving them out?

Skills

Have you presented your skills in the language of potential employers, in terminology appropriate to your goals?

Have you been objective and thorough in your self-assessment, presenting skills you truly possess and those you feel confident using on the job?

Have you provided evidence concerning where you developed and utilized these skills, referring to experiences, education, and activities?

Qualifications summary

Have you outlined the qualifications you possess, those that would be attractive to an employer considering you for a position related to your Objective?

Do you demonstrate an understanding of the target career field by using appropriate terminology and stressing appropriate characteristics?

Have you considered using headings such as Languages, Publications, or Related Experience to highlight important information?

Extracurricular and community activities

Have you listed appropriate activities, noting leadership positions and describing responsibilities?

If you included organizations that might be controversial, have you considered how a potential employer might react?

Have you presented activities in a clear manner, avoiding acronyms and describing little-known organizations and awards?

Interests

Have you included only positive information, leaving out anything that can be viewed negatively?

Personal data

If presented, did you leave out any information that could be used to discriminate against you?

References

If you listed references on your resume, did you include name, title, organization, address, and phone number for each reference?

Did you present a statement concerning availability of references or supplemental materials? Have you made sure that your references will be readily available?

If you developed a separate list of references, matching your resume, did you list name, title, organization, and phone number for each reference?

ORDER OF ELEMENTS

Are the most important topics first?

If your resume is more than one page, is the most important information on the first page?

If you have developed more than one resume, have you considered the order of appearance for each?

OVERALL PRESENTATION

Is your resume well organized, presenting a professional image, highlighting the most important information?

Can you elaborate on all elements of your resume if called upon to do so in an interview?

Does your resume present your qualifications in the best light possible, stressing skills?

Does your resume make it easy for a potential employer to say yes to a request for an interview?

Is your resume concise and thorough?

Is your resume the most professional presentation of your ability to complete a task effectively and successfully?

Would you be proud to show a potential employer your resume?

Production Techniques

Resumes can be typed or professionally typeset, or they can be produced by word processing. They can be traditional—laid out on standard 8½-by-11-inch white paper—or innovative, with designs that incorporate various graphic techniques and make use of unusual paper sizes. What is important is that you realize that you are in control of the resume-writing process. There is no one right way to produce a resume; you must decide on the contents and format that will suit you best.

The information on your Chronological Flowchart, Skills Inventory, Skills Flowchart, and Job Target Chart helped you decide what to include on your resume and how to present it, and the sample resumes showed you how a number of job seekers sold their liberal arts power through effective uses of certain topics and formats. If you're still uncertain about how to design your resume, reread the analyses that accompany each sample to learn why specific categories appear and why a particular format was chosen.

The two most important factors to keep in mind are the quality of the final document and the cost.

As the sample resumes illustrate, you can achieve excellent results with either typing or typesetting. The two most important factors to keep in mind are the quality of the final duplication-ready document and the cost.

Typing

If you are going to type your resume, you must do so using a high-quality electronic business typewriter. Do not use a portable or manual model; the poor quality will show up in the duplicated copies. The better the typewriter, the crisper the finished version.

Some typewriters come equipped with various typing elements or "daisywheels" that enable you to use different type styles such as italic or boldface for highlighting purposes. These kinds of typewriters can be rented for approximately $50 to $75 a month.

Instead of typing your resume yourself, you may want to have it typed. Before agreeing to anything, however, ask to see a sample of the typist's work as well as samples of the various typing styles available. The cost of having a resume professionally typed varies, ranging in most cases from $7 to $15 per page.

Typesetting

Typesetting is the process of setting copy in type, usually so that it can be printed on a press, as is done with books. Using this method can result in a very professional and distinctive-looking resume, and it gives you the option of choosing from a wide variety of typefaces for headings and text. Resumes that are typeset can make an impression of creativity or conservatism, depending on

If you can locate a typesetting service that is reasonable in price or if you have access to a personal computer and laser printer, I strongly encourage you to use this approach.

the type style and layout. Professional typesetting can be an expensive process, though, ranging in price from $25 to $40 per typeset page, duplication costs not included. With the coming of desktop publishing, using computers, word processing and graphics software, and laser printers, it is now difficult to differentiate between the more traditional photo-offset typesetting and computer-driven typesetting. In fact, most printing services use the computer method to develop duplication-ready copy. The newer process allows easier and quicker corrections, more efficient storage of copy, and can be, as detailed a bit later, available to individual resume writers through personal computers. If you can locate a typesetting service that is reasonable in price or if you have access to a personal computer and laser printer, I strongly encourage you to use this approach.

Another important thing to keep in mind is that having your resume typeset is one way of condensing it if you need to; a page and a half of typewritten copy can be reduced to one page or less, depending on the typeface used. The difference in cost between duplicating a one-page resume and a two-page resume might make typesetting a more attractive option.

Word Processing and Printing

Word processing is the use of a typewriter with a memory or a computer with word processing software. When a resume is typed—entered—on a word processor, the finished version is stored on tape or on a disk and is then retrievable at any time. To duplicate your resume, you simply locate it on the storage device and instruct the machine to print. A printer is either impact, inkjet, or laser, using keys, daisywheels, or pins; ink projection devices; or thermal processes, respectively. As stated, laser-printed resumes are, in most cases, equal in quality to typeset resumes.

More and more students have access to word processing, through either college and university mainframe and microcomputer facilities or their own personal computers. Given the fact that you can make corrections easily and quickly and then store the latest version of your resume indefinitely, this is an option that you should try to take advantage of. You can change objective statements as needed and rework the format and layout of your resume in minutes. If you have a choice of word processing equipment and software, determine whether you can change type styles and size, whether shadow-printing or bolding capabilities are available, and how easy it is to make changes and retrieve copy. Make sure that the system is equipped with a letter-quality daisywheel or, preferably, laser printer. Dot-matrix impact printers are not acceptable for creating duplication-ready resumes, although they can, if of good quality, be used for some job search correspondence.

As most students (and nonstudents) have gained access to personal computers, this has become the method of choice for producing duplication-ready copies of a resume. It offers the most flexibility and can, if the proper printer is used, offer the highest quality at the lowest cost. Obviously, I recommend this as the best method to produce your resume.

Photo-offset Printing vs. Photocopying

Photo-offset is a printing process that involves making a photographic negative of the camera-ready copy, which has been either typed or typeset. The negative is made into a plate that is then used on a printing press.

Photocopying is a process of duplicating by means of a wet or dry chemical transfer. Almost all of us are accustomed to using photocopiers.

A few years ago I strongly recommended that all job seekers have their resumes printed by the photo-offset process. Now, although I occasionally suggest offset printing, I more strongly recommend that resume writers explore the option of photocopying. Because offset printing is a true printing process it creates a very crisp duplication. Advances in photocopying equipment, however, have made it possible to produce copies that are indistinguishable from printed versions, but not all photocopying services have the proper equipment. Photocopying can result in copies that have toner residue, with shadows or spots appearing on resumes. If you use a professional copy service you can, in most cases, feel confident about the quality of duplication. Also, these businesses usually sell blank sheets of paper and envelopes that match your resume.

Do NOT use coin-operated photocopiers like the ones in libraries. The paper in these machines is not high quality and your resume will not create a very positive impression. NEVER use a wet paper copier, with slick chemical paper, to duplicate your resume. Before you decide on a photo-offset or photocopying service, ask to see samples of work they have done. Photocopy services can immediately show you how your resume will turn out. If you judge the quality of the photocopy acceptable—clean and crisp—you may wish to use this technique because it is usually much quicker and less expensive.

You MUST have your resume printed on high-quality bond paper.

Photo-offset copying varies in cost, from $15 to $50 for 100 copies of a one-page resume, so it is important that you shop around for the best price. The price of offset and photocopying will be influenced by the type of paper your resume is printed on. You must have your resume printed on high-quality bond paper. Use a bond with some cotton fiber and texture. Photocopying on good-quality paper will range from 10 cents to 25 cents per page; thus 100 copies of a one-page photocopied resume would be $10 to $25. Sometimes offset printing is more expensive and other times photocopying is more expensive. You must get price estimates before selecting a duplication service.

Even if you have access to a word processor, it is suggested that you not type an original resume for each employer. You should be involved in too many other job search activities to make this feasible. Time spent at the keyboard and printer should be spent on developing effective job search correspondence and preparing for interviews. Employers understand that resumes are duplicated, but they do expect the duplication to be of the best quality.

How Many Copies Should You Have?

It is better to have too many copies than too few. I suggest you have at least 50 copies of your resume, even if you have more than one resume, and that you obtain an estimate on the cost of 100 copies. As discussed earlier, the resume is your way of initiating and maintaining communications with potential employers and resource persons as well as a tool to use throughout the interview process. Having 50 to 100 resumes on hand will mean that you'll always be ready to take advantage of a new opportunity. You should distribute your resume to as many people as possible. You will never be an' effective job hunter if you are too possessive of your resume.

Paper

Whether photocopied or photo-offset printed, your resume must be duplicated on high-quality bond paper. Choose a conservative businesslike color; white, ivory, or off-white are perhaps the best. Beige or gray may be appropriate for more creative resumes or for contacting nontraditional employers, but bright colors should be avoided. The content of your resume and cover letters, not the color of the paper they are printed on, is what needs to stand out. Again, do not duplicate your resume on plain paper from a photocopier, and avoid parchmentlike erasable paper.

It is a good idea to purchase blank pages and envelopes of the same paper your resume is printed on to use for cover letters and additional correspondence. Some job seekers have stationery printed to match their resume, with the same type used for name and address. The total presentation of the resume, stationery, and envelope as a matching set projects a strong, positive image.

Do Some Comparison Shopping, Then Decide

As you can tell from the previous discussion, the cost of developing a finished version and of duplicating a resume will vary from technique to technique, and the range of possible costs is quite wide. I strongly suggest that you get estimates from at least three duplication or printing services before you make a final choice. Consult the yellow pages and contact the career planning and placement office of your school for suggestions. Some career planning and placement facilities are able to recommend typists, typesetters, and printers. Also ask for advice from counselors and others who have already completed their resumes.

Some Ways to Save Money

Some colleges and universities have good-quality typewriters available for use by students. Ask around and locate one. If you can type your own finished version—without errors—you will save

Distribute copies of your resume to as many people as possible. You will never be an effective job hunter if you are too possessive of your resume.

The content of your resume and cover letters, not the color of the paper they are printed on, is what needs to stand out.

some money. Sometimes clerical staff people want to earn a little extra money by typing or word processing resumes. These people may charge less than professional typists.

Some school newspapers have typesetting equipment. Ask if you can use this equipment or if you can have your resume typeset for a minimal charge.

More and more college and university computer centers make word processing available to students through mainframe computers and microcomputers. Also, more and more students have their own microcomputers with word processing software as well as access to high-quality printers. You may use this equipment to develop a finished version or to duplicate your resume, as well as to write cover letters to potential employers. If you use a word processor to duplicate your resume, you will have to purchase paper. This can be done through printers, stationery stores, or printing suppliers. Shop around to get the best price on paper, and don't forget envelopes.

The cost of duplicating your resume could be significantly lower if you provide the paper.

Even if you are not using a word processor, you may wish to purchase your own paper. The cost of duplicating your resume could be significantly lower if you provide the paper. If you are thinking about this, obtain estimates of what photocopying and photo-offset printing would cost if you supplied the paper.

College and university printing offices—not frequently used by students but often available to them—sometimes have excellent prices for students. Explore this option.

The key to saving money is preliminary research. Take the extra time to shop around and be an informed consumer.

Job Search Correspondence

Cover Letters

When you are making initial contact with a potential employer by mail, your resume MUST be accompanied by a cover letter. There is simply no excuse for not sending one. Many employers report that they won't even look at a resume that comes without at least a few lines of explanation.

Resumes can tell potential employers only what you have done. Cover letters can tell them why you became involved in particular activities, what you gained from the experiences, and, more important, why you are writing to them and what it is about your resume that they should pay particular attention to. Cover letters allow you to cite accomplishments that would be of special interest to a given employer and to elaborate on specific sections of your resume. Time and time again I am told by recruiters that cover letters are just as important as resumes when applicants are making initial contact by mail. Therefore, cover letters must be as powerful as resumes. They must be able to stand alone, independent of the resume, and be effective enough to ignite interest in your candidacy. If your resume and cover letter were reviewed separately, by different people, each piece of correspondence must project your qualifications in a way that would make the reviewer want to recommend you for an interview. Of course, rarely are cover letters sent or reviewed without resumes, but all correspondence should be powerful, independent documents. When combined, the total effect of these job search parts should be more than twice as powerful as the sum of the individual effects. Cover letters can in many cases determine whether you are granted an interview. Even if you plan to contact a potential employer by phone, send a cover letter first to present your background and questions and to prepare the employer for your call.

The sample cover letters on pages 130 to 136 are NOT meant to be copied word for word. Any correspondence with a potential employer must be yours; it must project your writing style and personality. The samples are meant to guide and motivate you as you undertake your own job search actions. They illustrate various approaches that liberal arts job seekers may take when making initial contact with employers. (Refer to Joseph E. Byrne's resume on page 48 to better understand how his cover letters advance his interests.)

Cover letters may also function as letters of inquiry when you are contacting potential employers to determine the hiring needs of an

Cover letters are just as important as resumes when applicants are making initial contact by mail.

organization or as letters of application when you are responding to specific job advertisements. Cover letters should be used to:

- Introduce yourself and to present your reasons for contacting the employer;

- Draw attention to your resume and to highlight specific qualifications;

- Inform the employer that you will be contacting him or her soon;

- Request information from someone who works in a field you are interested in.

There are several accepted formats for business correspondence, and cover letters should be written using one of them. The illustration of the components of a cover letter on page 130 shows one of several standard styles.

Cover letters should always be addressed to the person who is responsible for initiating the review process or for making the ultimate hiring decision. Avoid sending your letters to "To Whom It May Concern," "Dear Sir or Madam," or "Personnel Director." Make a phone call or two to find out the name and title of the individual you should contact and to confirm the address of the hiring organization. College career services offices may have current names of recruiters for organizations of interest; membership directories of national or regional personnel associations can also be very useful.

While the earlier advice is still appropriate in a majority of cases, the advent of facsimile reproduction (fax) and overnight delivery systems has added a few new weapons to the job seeker's arsenal and a few new twists to job search strategies. If you have access to a fax machine, you may wish to use it to transmit your initial correspondence, after calling to determine who should receive it. This will speed up the process and allow you the security of knowing that you can make follow-up phone calls immediately. Also, if you believe that time is a critical factor, invest the extra money in sending information via overnight delivery. Again, this will allow you to follow up after the stated delivery time confident that your letter arrived. Of course, this can get expensive if you are communicating with a number of employers, but don't forget this option for the instances when it can increase the power of your actions.

Follow-up Letters

A job search is, obviously, an ongoing communications process, not limited to the initial contact and, if one is lucky, the interview. The best job seekers are the most assertive and powerful communicators, not passive applicants. Therefore, it is appropriate to maintain ongoing communications with potential employers by follow-up actions. Traditionally, a job search communication pattern is an alternating series of letters and phone calls, with in-person visits included. Once you believe an employer has received your initial correspondence, call to see if you can arrange an interview. After the interview, follow with a thank-you note and, a bit later, a phone call to determine the status of the decision-making process. Occasionally, after receiving a rejection, you can follow up with a letter expressing disappointment but appreciation for the consideration; you can also try to get additional information that will help you determine what to do next.

Everything a potential employer receives from you must project your liberal arts power, your ultimate power to perform on the job.

As in any relationship, you must be sensitive to issues related to the people you interact with during your job search. You want to be assertive, but not aggressive—persistent, yet polite. Generally, if you are businesslike in your communications (phone, letter, or in person), you will do fine. There may be situations when you have to wait a few weeks until you contact someone again and others when you should do so immediately. The secret is to always ask when and how the next communication should be made and who should initiate it. If you have been told it is all right to call after a few days, then you should feel comfortable doing so.

As your job search goes on, you should take an occasional retrospective look at your efforts. Follow up with persons you have already contacted, including your references, informing them of your efforts and seeking advice and counsel. By rekindling old contacts, by phone or mail, you may be taking an action that could recharge your job search. Examples of follow-up letters appear on pages 137 and 138. As with the sample cover letters, they are meant to illustrate possibilities, not to be copied. You may wish to refer to Jordan Alna's resume and job search success story on pages 46 and 97 to better understand how these letters fit into the context of job search actions.

All job search correspondence, like resumes, illustrates the nature of work you can do for a potential employer. Pay close attention to style and format. All written correspondence should be typed (or word processed) on good-quality paper, free of errors and erasures. All letters should have correct addresses and phone numbers and be properly signed. Everything a potential employer receives from you—resume, cover letter, follow-up letter, or supporting materials—must project your liberal arts power, your ultimate power to perform on the job.

The elements of a cover letter.

```
                                        Your Street Address
                                        City, State Zip Code
                                        The Date
[Space down four spaces.]

Ms. Betty Wilson
Director
Recruiting and Staffing
Jefferson Industries, Inc.
9463 East Broad Street
Richmond, Virginia 23261

Dear Ms. Wilson:

The opening paragraph should state why you are writing and why you are
interested in the organization. If you are writing a letter of
application, you should name the position for which you are applying
and tell the employer how you became aware of it. A letter of inquiry
should provide evidence of your career-mindedness; it helps to refer
to specific job functions, if not titles. If you were referred to the
employer by a career counselor, a former employer, or an aunt, this is
the best place to mention that person's name and to point out that he
or she suggested you write.

The middle paragraph is where you draw attention to your resume and
highlight specific skills relevant to the potential employer. Present
your motives for seeking employment with this organization and cite
achievements and qualifications related to the position desired. If
you have qualifications that are not noted on your resume, this is
your opportunity to discuss them.

The closing paragraph states what you will do next (such as calling to
arrange an interview at the employer's convenience) or what you would
like the recipient of the letter to do next. An assertive statement
explaining what you plan to do and what you hope the employer will do
is harder to ignore than a vague request for consideration.

Sincerely,

[Signature Here]

Your Name Typed

Enclosure [This indicates that your resume or additional materials are
enclosed.]
```

A pre-interview letter. This letter can be used to contact an on-campus recruiter in order to initiate interest prior to the campus visit. It can also be used to arrange a special interview if the recruiter's schedule is filled. An advance letter shows sales initiative and gives the recruiter a bit more time to judge an applicant's qualifications.

3877 University
Austin, Texas 78712
September 18, 1989

Mr. Lawrence Brooks
Manager
Corporate Recruiting
Procter & Gamble
P.O. Box 836
Cincinnati, Ohio 45201

Dear Mr. Brooks:

I am looking forward to your visit to the University of Texas at the beginning of next month. As I told you this morning on the phone, I will be graduating from UT this May and would very much like to work for Procter & Gamble as a Field Sales Representative.

My greatest strengths are in marketing ideas and services. Through a number of employment and extracurricular experiences I have gained a great deal of experience organizing, promoting, and publicizing events. I know that I can sell and that I can provide the sales support required of professional Field Sales Representatives. If by some chance I am unable to schedule an interview with you through our placement office, I will give you a call while you are on campus to see if we can get together at a convenient time to discuss my qualifications.

I am very interested in Procter & Gamble and sincerely hope that we can meet during your recruiting trip. Thank you for your consideration.

Sincerely,

Anne Marie Sonselle

Anne Marie Sonselle

Enclosure

A sample letter of application. Sidestepping an employer's stated preference for a marketing major, Anne Marie presents her qualifications in active and assertive terms.

3877 University
Austin, Texas 78712
March 26, 1990

Mr. Stephen P. Tatoe
Manager of College Relations
Frito-Lay
P.O. Box 741
Dallas, Texas 75235

Dear Mr. Tatoe:

I read the letter you recently sent to the Career Planning and Placement Office of the University of Texas College of Business Administration. I am writing to say that I would like to be considered for employment in Frito-Lay's marketing department. I will be graduating from the University of Texas this May, and I would very much like to begin a career in sales and marketing with your organization.

You will note from the enclosed resume that many of my extracurricular and work experiences involved the organization, promotion, and publicizing of events. I have had direct sales experience soliciting potential customers for We Three Caterers and have been successful in managing employees in various capacities. Perhaps the most challenging and rewarding experience I have had to date was working with Congressman Gradison and the organizing committee of the University of Texas Literary Festival. I am confident that I have the sales and managerial skills required to be a contributing member of the Frito-Lay organization.

A letter and resume can tell you only so much about my motivations and qualifications. I would welcome the opportunity to discuss my background with you in person and would travel to Dallas at my own expense to do so. I will call you at the end of next week to discuss whether such a meeting would be possible and to confirm appropriate next steps.

Thank you for your consideration.

Sincerely,

Anne Marie Sonselle

Anne Marie Sonselle

Enclosure

A letter of inquiry. By being creative and using an old newspaper want ad to uncover a potential job opening, Anne Marie might uncover a diamond in the rough.

3877 University
Austin, Texas 78712
April 2, 1990

Mrs. Carey Washington
Director of Personnel
Mattel Toys
3876 Rosecrans Avenue
Hawthorne, California 90250

Dear Mrs. Washington:

While reviewing past editions of the <u>Wall Street Journal</u>, I came across an advertisement you placed concerning an opening for a sales representative. I am sure that this particular post has been filled, but I am writing to ask whether another position has opened up since then.

Upon graduation from the University of Texas this May, I would like to begin a career in sales with an organization such as Mattel Toys. Many of my extracurricular and work experiences, detailed in the enclosed resume, involved organizing, promoting, and publicizing events. I have had direct sales experience at We Three Caterers. Perhaps the most challenging and rewarding were my experiences with Congressman Gradison and the University of Texas Literary Festival. I know that I can sell, and I know that I am capable of providing the sales support required of successful sales representatives.

I look forward to hearing from you concerning possible opportunities. Thank you for your consideration.

Sincerely,

Anne Marie Sonselle

Anne Marie Sonselle

Enclosure

A request for an informational interview.

                                        Box 1222
                                        Tulane University
                                        New Orleans, LA 70118
                                        February 19, 1990

Mr. James L. Throser
Blane, Collier, and Phips
Suite 3987
One Shell Square
New Orleans, LA 70118

Dear Mr. Throser:

I am writing on the recommendation of Joan Webster, the Director of Career Planning and Placement at Tulane University. Ms. Webster and I have discussed my interest in the field of law, and she suggested that since you are an alumnus of both Tulane University and the Tulane School of Law, you might be willing to offer some advice and provide me with information about the best way to prepare for a career in law. I have enclosed a copy of my resume to familiarize you with my background.

At present I am looking for a position as a paralegal or legal assistant. It is my intention to gain some exposure to legal work and learn some of the fundamental skills required of a lawyer before applying to law school one or two years down the road. I would be interested in your thoughts concerning this strategy and, of course, would welcome any assistance or advice you could provide.

I understand how busy you are, so I will come with specific questions about the legal profession. I will call your office to arrange an appointment at your convenience.

Thank you for your consideration.

Sincerely,

Joseph E. Byrne

Joseph E. Byrne

Enclosure

A letter of inquiry. Using a lead gained through an informational interview, Joseph writes to inquire about possible job openings.

Box 1222
Tulane University
New Orleans, LA 70118
March 12, 1990

Ms. Lane Brenden
Orin and Thayer
Suite 777
One Shell Square
New Orleans, LA 70118

Dear Ms. Brenden:

I am writing on the recommendation of James Throser of Blane, Collier, and Phips. Mr. Throser and I have discussed my interest in the legal profession and my current efforts to locate a law-related position.

As noted on the enclosed resume, I would like to use my research and writing skills in a law office after graduating from Tulane in December. My courses have required me to undertake a great many research projects and write many papers. Enclosed you will find a few abstracts of my efforts. They are intended to illustrate my capacity to do research and report findings in appropriate formats. I understand that these are skills that are required of paralegals and legal assistants.

I work well under the pressure of deadlines, and I am used to paying close attention to detail. I have had experience working as part of a team, and I have come to learn that one must work extremely hard in order to achieve success. I am willing and able to do so for Orin and Thayer.

Are there any openings for paralegals or legal assistants in your firm at the present time?

I will call you the week of March 19 to discuss employment opportunities with Orin and Thayer. Thank you very much for your consideration.

Sincerely,

Joseph E. Byrne

Joseph E. Byrne

Enclosures

A letter of application. Used to respond to a job posting, this letter highlights skills and motivation while demonstrating the applicant's ability to write a good business letter.

Box 1222
Tulane University
New Orleans, LA 70118
April 2, 1990

Ms. Marie Jeannette
Paralegal Manager
Daley, Daley, and Rogers
200 Park Avenue
New York, NY 10166

Dear Ms. Jeannette:

I am writing to apply for the paralegal position that was posted in the Tulane University Career Planning and Placement office. The position described in your posting seems to match my career goals and qualifications.

As noted on the enclosed resume, I would like to utilize my research and writing skills while working for a law firm as a paralegal. My academic courses have required a great many research projects and papers. Enclosed are a few abstracts of my efforts. I hope they demonstrate to you my capacity to undertake research and report findings in a clear and concise fashion.

I can work well under the pressure of deadlines, and I have been involved in a great many group projects. My work experiences have taught me that one must be prepared to work beyond the typical 40-hour week to achieve success. I am willing and able to do so for Daley, Daley, and Rogers.

Your active consideration of my credentials would be greatly appreciated. I will call you on Friday to confirm receipt of this letter and to discuss appropriate next steps. Please feel free to contact me if you require additional information to support my candidacy.

Thank you.

Sincerely,

Joseph E. Byrne

Joseph E. Byrne

Enclosures

A sample follow-up letter.

Doane Hall, Box A11
Denison University
Granville, Ohio 43023
February 5, 1990

Ms. Rea Cruter
College Relations Manager
Baxter Healthcare Corporation
One Baxter Parkway
Deerfield, Illinois 60015

Dear Ms. Cruter:

It has been a while since we met at the Denison University Career Planning and Placement Office. Although disappointed that our initial conversation did not result in my being asked back for additional interviews, I remain very, very interested in Baxter Healthcare Corporation.

Since our meeting I have developed a new resume, one which better presents my goals and capabilities, and I have done a great deal of thinking about why I wish to work for your organization. Like any good salesperson, I have learned from rejections and remain undaunted in my desire to successfully market my product--me.

I draw your attention to the Qualifications and Capabilities section of my resume. Here I have identified the varied yet significant experiences that have enabled me to develop skills required of a successful salesperson, specifically a salesperson who works within the health-care industry. I possess

- *the organizational abilities to effectively manage my time and ultimately the time and efforts of others;*
- *the academic framework, research skills, and curiosity required to understand products and the needs of the customer;*
- *the health-care background and the communication and persuasive skills needed to develop effective relationships and present information in appropriate ways; and*
- *the persistence and tenacity required to follow up until actions yield results.*

While your judgment of my candidacy may have been accurate at the time of our first meeting, I sincerely believe I am better prepared now for a truer assessment of my capabilities. I would like to meet with you again or with one of your colleagues at Baxter. Of course, I would be willing to travel to Chicago or one of your regional offices at my own expense.

I will call you soon to speak with you regarding your reactions to this request. Thank you for your continued consideration.

Sincerely,

Jordan Elizabeth Alna

Jordan Elizabeth Alna

Enclosure

Follow-up after a rejection.

Doane Hall, Box A11
Denison University
Granville, Ohio 43023
March 7, 1990

Mr. Justin Blake
Manager of College Relations and
  Professional Employment
Merck & Company, Inc.
Box 2000
Rahway, New Jersey 07065

Dear Mr. Blake:

As per our recent phone conversation, I do understand that
reconsideration of my candidacy is not a possibility at present, and I
will communicate again later in the spring. I certainly appreciate
your offering to provide me with the name of Merck's regional sales
representative for the Little Rock area. Once I have received this
information, I will contact this person to arrange an informational
interview while back home over spring break. The more people I meet
and the more I understand about the field of pharmaceutical and
health-care sales, the more likely it is that I will obtain my goal.
Upon my return to campus in early April, I will let you know how the
conversation went.

Your assistance and consideration to date are very much appreciated.
Thank you.

Sincerely,

Jordan Alna

Jordan Alna

The Resume and the Interview

We have, throughout this book, defined liberal arts power as a blending of ability, attitude, and actions. We have also defined it as the taking of responsibility by liberal arts majors for communicating goals and qualifications and as taking *response-ability* to develop powerful job search tools and strategies. The development of powerful resumes and job search correspondence has already been discussed. Now let's explore how one can be most effective during the employment interview, ultimately the most important job search action and another indication of one's response-ability. Developing liberal arts powerful interview skills involves thinking of the employment interview as a *communications* process, not as an *application* process. You do not apply for a job; you communicate to a potential employer the qualifications you possess to perform on the job. Communications skills are among the strongest of those possessed by liberal arts students, so an effective interviewee simply applies these skills in a special way. Your responsibility is now most literally your response-ability, your ability to respond effectively to questions as well as situations.

The Four P's

The liberal arts powerful interviewee knows the four P's.

Preparation

Know your interests, skills, and capabilities. Be able to discuss how you developed these characteristics—through course work, part-time or full-time employment, or volunteer or extracurricular activities—and where you used them to accomplish tasks. You may wish to use the exercises that appeared earlier in this book to document your personal qualities. Even if you developed a functional resume, it's a good idea to review your Skills Inventory and Skills Flowchart prior to an interview.

Read your own resume before an interview! Be prepared to discuss key points you believe highlight your qualifications. The Pre-Interview Resume Exercise that appears in the Appendix requires you to review your resume prior to an interview and provides some useful guidelines for organizing your thoughts. To complete this exercise, use your Job Target Chart if the stated Fields and Job Titles on the chart match the ones you are interviewing for. Whatever the case, the Pre-Interview Resume Exercise is an excellent way to prepare for an interview. You may wish to complete one prior to each interview and take it with you for last-minute review.

Be able to articulate your goals. This does not mean predicting the future or knowing exactly where you will be in five years. It means that you should be able to discuss the functions you wish to perform on the job and the possible directions you might take. This comes from thorough research of jobs and potential employers.

Be familiar with your work experiences, paid and volunteer. Be able to discuss responsibilities and accomplishments in active terms. Be prepared to cite facts and figures, if appropriate. Again, the exercises that you completed to develop your resume and the Pre-Interview Resume Exercise should prove extremely valuable in helping you document and recall important data.

Know your strengths and weaknesses. We all have them! Discuss your strengths and cite examples of how you make them work for you. A good strategy to use when discussing your weaknesses is to mention ways in which you are trying to improve—and what strengths you use to compensate for your weaknesses.

Research the organization as thoroughly as possible. Include recruiting literature (developed by the organization and containing discussions of job functions, career paths, and general corporate information), corporate literature (annual reports and descriptions of products or services), and periodical literature (appearing in newspapers, magazines, or journals) in your research. College or university career services facilities and the reference librarian of a business or general library are helpful in locating these resources. Don't be afraid to ask the organization for information; your research does not have to be done in secret. When you are arranging an interview, ask if you can get information about the job and firm. Try to give yourself enough time between the request for an interview and the actual interview date to conduct your research. When it comes time for the interview you should be knowledgeable about the company's history, geographic locations, general methods of doing business, reputation, proposed growth or redirection, organizational structure (particularly of the department where you wish to work), and recent events of particular note. Know the functions for which you are interviewing and be prepared to state why you are interested in a particular job and organization in terms of what you can do for the organization, not what it can do for you.

Call friends, family members, and alumni (if you have access to listings through career planning and placement offices) who might know something about the organization or about the persons you will be interviewing with. The more you know, the more powerful an interviewee you will be.

Prepare some appropriate and thoughtful questions to ask. You may wish to ask about day-to-day job functions, the atmosphere within which you will be working, the people you will be working with, what directions the position and firm might take, and what the corporate culture is like.

Presence

Personal appearance and behavior are very important. The way you dress, speak, act, the way you carry yourself, all are part of the image you project to an employer. It is this image that an interviewer judges. A general rule of thumb is to dress as if you were working for the organization while erring on the side of being a bit overdressed or conservative. A positive personality can overcome a bland dress or suit, but if your clothing speaks too loudly, what you say about yourself might not be heard.

Be aware of body language and posture, but don't worry about every gesture or movement. Find a comfortable position that allows you to face the interviewer and express yourself in effective ways. Remember that eye contact can enhance communication, but don't stare. Avoid mannerisms that indicate tension or nervousness (easier said than done), and be natural when using hand, body, and facial gestures.

Avoid slang and trite phrases. Use proper grammar and a varied vocabulary. When appropriate, use phrases that are specific to the job for which you are interviewing. Speak clearly and audibly. Maintain a positive attitude, and express confidence (without being arrogant) in your ability to perform the tasks associated with the position. Don't dwell on negatives or overly criticize situations or persons, particularly past employers. If you do speak about these people or situations, do so in an intelligent and analytical manner.

Be honest and sincere. By being yourself you are giving the interviewer the best opportunity to judge whether a match exists.

Participation

Be an active listener and responsible (response-able) participant, not a passive respondent. Elaborate on answers when appropriate. Show that you are listening by means of head nods and making brief statements that reflect understanding. Make references to earlier answers and, of course, to your resume. Use the resume as the common document that you and the interviewer share. It can be a menu of potential interview topics that each of you can choose from. Paraphrase and summarize to remind the interviewer of important points. Be sure to ask questions if you need more information.

Present your qualifications in terms of interests, skills, and values, paralleling the criteria for the position. Use specific details and cite examples. Don't leave it up to interviewers to make connections between statements on your resume and qualifications for a position. Sharing insights into your values and what motivates you to perform will powerfully project your abilities and attitudes in this critical job search action.

Ask for clarification of vague or "open-ended" questions. Use this opportunity to bring up favorable information that has not yet been discussed. Don't panic.

Answer questions by highlighting abilities, attitudes, and accomplishments, by projecting liberal arts power. You share control of the interview with the interviewer. If you leave an interview without sharing information that can be used to judge your qualifications, it is not because you were not asked the "right" questions but because you did not take advantage of the opportunity to powerfully present your qualifications. Come into each interview with a strategy and predetermined key points (remember the Pre-Interview Resume Exercise) while being as flexible as you can and flowing with the interview as it takes form.

Poise

Preparation, the first P, and practice, the unspoken fifth P, equal poise. Practice will enable you to be more and more comfortable in an interview situation. Do not use actual interviews for practice. Whenever you interview, you should sincerely want to receive an offer, or, at the very least, be able to determine whether the job is right for you. Practice with a counselor, with a friend, or alone. Use a tape recorder or videotape recorder, if possible. Lists of typical interview questions appear in numerous publications. You can use such a list to structure practice sessions.

Maintain your composure in trying situations. You may have to wait a long time for an interviewer. The interviewer may receive phone calls during the interview. The interviewer might have a stressful style. Keep in control!

Remember, there is no such thing as a "blown" interview. Although a particular interview may not result in a job offer, or even additional consideration, subsequent communication and follow-up can lead to additional information and, on occasion, revive your candidacy.

Ending and Following the Interview

Conclude an interview with some understanding as to where you stand, what might happen next, and who should contact whom and when.

Follow the interview with a thank-you note. This gesture might not get you the job, but it can't hurt. You can use this as an opportunity to summarize what was said in the interview or to add points that were not discussed. In addition, don't be afraid to make follow-up phone calls if you haven't heard from an interviewer in an agreed-upon time period. Be persistent, patient, and polite in your attempts to follow up with a potential employer.

Types of Interviews and Interviewers

There are various types of interviews, each requiring a somewhat different approach. The first interview, often a screening interview, is different from a call-back or selection interview. An interview on campus is different from one at the potential employer's office and different from one at an employment agency. Interviews in which the interviewer has reviewed a great deal of information about you (such as call-back interviews) are different from those in which the interviewer knows very little (such as on-campus or screening interviews).

Just as there are different types of interviews, there are different types of interviewers. Some ask typical questions, others have a more open and conversational style, while some pressure you for answers to difficult questions and create a "stress interview." Others spend a great deal of time talking about their organization, rather than addressing your background. The powerful, and thus successful, interviewee will react well to whatever occurs because of thorough preparation and the liberal arts abilities to adapt and react.

On-Site Interviews

Because follow-up, on-site interviews are critical to your getting an offer, the following tips provide more specific information.

Do background reading, again. In addition to reading an annual report and company literature, do some "current events" reading, reviewing articles dealing with the company and career field. Of course, know what position you are being considered for and what determining factors might be. Remember, those who interview you, and there will most likely be several at this stage, will have reviewed your resume and the reports of anyone who has already met you, so you must also review your resume. Be prepared to state why you are interested in the organization and position and have specific examples of how you would apply your skills to the job in question.

Prior to any interview that requires travel, inquire about travel arrangements and reimbursement procedures. Organizations often have different ways of making arrangements and reimbursing you for expenses. You should know before the interview, if possible, what these procedures involve. Do not abuse expense reimbursements; travel as if you already work for the organization, mindful of costs. Whenever possible, obtain an agenda of your interview day before the interview, and if you have any concerns, contact the person who is coordinating your visit.

Be prepared for a long day of interviews. Take your fatigue factor into account when scheduling interviews. Although it is convenient to schedule interviews with more than one organization if they are headquartered in the same city, do not spread yourself too thin. Be rested for your interviews, and keep your energy level high throughout the day.

Be consistent. Don't be a chameleon, changing your answers for each person you see. Sincerity and honesty are essential. Everyone you interview with will compare notes at the end of your interviews. Be prepared to have the same questions asked by more than one interviewer. Be prepared for "what would you do in this situation" questions and have questions ready to ask your interviewers.

Be organized. Bring extra copies of your resume with you. Carry a small portfolio that can hold extra resumes, copies of correspondence with the organization, research notes and recruiting materials, a completed Pre-Interview Resume Exercise, a list of questions you would like to ask, travel and accommodations information, and notepaper. If the interviews are out of town, have enough cash and a credit card to deal with unexpected expenses you might encounter. Know who is coordinating your visit and feel free to contact that person if you have any problems or concerns or meet with unexpected delays.

Don't be surprised if you are asked to take a personality or aptitude test. Some organizations use these devices to determine whether you have traits they believe necessary for success. You might also be asked to sign documents related to your health status and willingness to undergo drug testing.

Salary and benefits issues may arise. It is appropriate to bring up these issues, preferably toward the end of the interview but ideally after an offer has been made. Be prepared to state what a realistic range might be or, if you are more experienced, exactly the compensation package you are looking for.

Postoffer analysis takes place after a job offer is received. Consult resource people and materials when you have reached this phase of your search. Feel free to ask difficult questions of your potential employer. The more information you have, the better the decision. Be prepared to work within an employer- or self-imposed time frame for decision making, but don't hesitate to ask for additional time if you need it.

The employment interview is perhaps the most important face-to-face communication you will have. Have confidence in your ability to become a powerful interviewee and to be successful at all phases of the job search. Make use of resources available—career services facilities, counselors, family members, friends, and others—to make you more powerful. You have the liberal arts power—the responsibility and response-ability—to be successful!

Closing Comments: Liberal Arts Power and You

It is my hope that this book has provided you, the liberal arts job seeker, with the information and motivation required to develop the very best, most powerful, resume possible. Although the contents are directed to the job search of liberal arts graduates, it was my intent to develop a resource that anyone, even non–liberal arts job seekers, could find of value. In closing, I would like to express a few additional, and perhaps more subjective, thoughts.

For you who do not want to add *ian, ist,* or *teacher* to the title of your major when asked, "What are you going to do with a major in . . . ?" or "What are you going to do after graduation?" by Uncle Harry in a rather taunting tone during Thanksgiving dinner at your grandparents' house, I wish the following:

- The *peace of mind* to ignore the questions and, if possible, the questioner, when appropriate to do so.

- The *patience* to bear with these questions until you are prepared to initiate the research and goal-setting process that will provide you with answers.

- The *persistence* required to complete this as well as the job search process that follows.

- The *power,* ultimately, to respond, citing your goals, sharing with the questioner a copy of your resume, and soliciting some suggested resources—turning an agitator into an ally.

I also offer you the promise that you possess all of the abilities and attitudes to complete the actions required to be a successful job seeker and a successful job performer. You are powerful! Once you are aware of this fact and have focused your power on resume writing and related job search efforts—on paper and in person—you will see for yourself.

Finally, in a sincere attempt to continue my own career development, which has allowed me to learn something from each of the thousands of job seekers I have counseled, I welcome your reactions to this edition (as well as suggestions for future ones) and personal stories of job search success. Please send your comments to me in care of Peterson's Guides. Rephrasing a traditional colloquialism, best wishes and more liberal arts power to you.

An Annotated Bibliography for Liberal Arts Majors

While the main purpose of this book is to initiate efforts required to develop a resume, it is hoped that you will set in motion actions that will result in research and job search goals that will lead to a liberal arts powerful job search strategy. The following resources include publications presenting information on numerous career fields, those with information on specific fields, and those providing information on the job search and on potential employers. Although lengthy, this is by no means an exhaustive listing. It is simply an overview of the types of materials that exist and the types of resources you should be using.

Basta, Nicholas. *Top Professions: The 100 Most Popular, Dynamic, and Profitable Careers in America Today.* Princeton, N.J.: Peterson's Guides, 1989.
Extensive market research by the author includes surveys of professional associations and interviews with key players in selected professions. Provides fresh, realistic guidance on the job market, uncovering promising options that are not widely publicized and guiding the reader in how to use current business and economic trends in making career decisions. Discusses average starting salaries, forecasts future demand, and provides contact numbers for professional associations.

Bestor, Dorothy. *Aside from Teaching, What in the World Can You Do?* Seattle: University of Washington Press, 1982.
A collection of essays dealing with career strategies for LA grads. Contains material drawn from author's experiences as teacher and counselor and from interviews and questionnaires. Extensive bibliography of career-related publications appears.

Calhoun, Mary. *How to Get the Hot Jobs in Business & Finance.* New York: Harper & Row, 1986.
Describes career options in business and finance throughout the country and gives job search advice. Lists potential employers.

Career Visions.
Monthly magazine containing information on many career fields. Offers job-hunting advice and addresses job advancement, career transition, and other relevant topics. Targets college students and recent college graduates, with copies available free on many campuses or for purchase at

newsstands. Career Visions, the publisher, also maintains Information Centers, which provide data on career fields and potential employers within major industry groupings, and periodically sponsors recruitment programs throughout the country.

Catalyst Career Opportunities Series. New York: Catalyst, 1985.
One of several publications that offers information on career fields and job hunting. Although written for women, these resources are of value to all. Titles include *Career Options, Educational Opportunities,* and *Career Opportunities.*

Collard, Betsy A. *The High-Tech Career Book: Finding Your Place in Today's Job Market.* Los Altos, Calif.: William Kaufman, 1986.
Breaks down the high-tech industry into functional areas including marketing, sales, materials management, finance and accounting, management information systems, human resources, writing, training, graphics, and public relations. Each area is discussed, including job roles and responsibilities, and job search advice is detailed. Includes sample want ads for positions discussed.

The Encyclopedia of Careers and Vocational Guidance. Chicago: Ferguson Publishing, 1987.
Three-volume publication with information on broad career fields and on specific jobs within these fields. Covers major industries and areas of work and contains articles on hundreds of occupations.

Figler, Howard. *The Complete Job-Search Handbook: All the Skills You Need to Get Any Job and Have a Good Time Doing It.* New York: Holt Rinehart and Winston, 1988.
Deals with the process of job hunting by discussing philosophy as well as process. You will need additional resources for information on specific fields and potential employers.

Flores-Esteves, Manuel. *Life After Shakespeare: Careers for Liberal Arts Majors.* New York: Penguin Books, 1985.
Discusses thirty fields that offer entry-level options for liberal arts job seekers, providing brief overviews and lists of additional field-related resources. Also contains brief resume and job search information.

Fowler, Elizabeth M. *The New York Times Career Planner.* New York: Times Books, 1987.
Contains information that originally appeared in Fowler's columns in the *New York Times.* Discusses some 100 options through field and job overviews, as well as job search, graduate school, and other career-related topics.

How to Get a Job in   . Chicago: Surrey Books.
Each title in this series of guides deals with job search in a specific major city, such as Chicago, Los Angeles, and Dallas/

Fort Worth. Each contains basic job-hunting information and lists potential employers by career fields. If your geographic goals match the cities covered by these books, they can be valuable resources.

The Job Finders. Englewood Cliffs, N.J.: Prentice-Hall.
A collection of books covering fields such as banking, data processing/information technology, public relations, publishing, and others. Partial listings of employers in each field; job search advice, including tips for writing resumes; and field-specific bibliographies.

Johnson's World Wide Chamber of Commerce Directory. Boulder, Colo.: Johnson Publishing, 1984.
Chamber of Commerce organizations publish and distribute listings of area employers. If you have clear geographic and functional goals, communications with these organizations are invaluable. This directory lists the officers and addresses of these organizations throughout the world.

Munschauer, John. *Jobs for English Majors and Other Smart People.* Rev. ed. Princeton, N.J.: Peterson's Guides, 1986.
Deals with job search issues for English majors and other liberal arts graduates. Shows job hunters how to spot needs that they can fill and gives down-to-earth advice on alternate routes to getting the right job.

Nadler, Burton Jay. *Liberal Arts Jobs: What They Are and How to Get Them.* 2nd ed. Princeton, N.J.: Peterson's Guides, 1989.
Geared to liberal arts majors, this book introduces concepts associated with the job search process, provides guidelines for successful goal setting, and offers information on more than 300 realistic job and career options.

Petras, Ross, and Kathryn Petras. *Inside Track: How to Get into and Succeed in America's Prestige Companies.* New York: Vantage Books, 1986.
Includes chapters on accounting, advertising, auction houses, automobiles, banks, corporate giants, entertainment, federal government, financial services, high tech, law, magazines, newspapers, public relations, publishing, retailing, and television. Gives information on the fields and potential employers, as well as a discussion on the cultural climates of the cited organizations.

Rosenthal, David, and Michael Powell. *Careers in Marketing.* Englewood Cliffs, N.J.: Prentice-Hall, 1984.
Covers the broad field of marketing, including marketing research, product management, advertising, sales, physical distribution, retailing, and nonprofit. Includes information on career paths and a bibliography.

Salzman, Marian. *Wanted: Liberal Arts Graduates.* New York: Doubleday, 1987.
Contains brief field overviews and highlights several

organizations offering entry-level programs. Also lists other organizations that can be contacted concerning potential employment.

Salzman, Marian, and Diedre Sullivan. *Inside Management Training.* New York: New American Library, 1985.
Covered are accounting, advertising, commercial banking, communications, computers and high technology, consumer products, hospitality, insurance, investment banking, management consulting, public service, and retailing. Includes brief field overviews and highlights several organizations offering entry-level programs. Also lists numerous other organizations that can be contacted concerning employment opportunities. Complete bibliography cites resources for each field, as well as general job search and interview skill information.

Scherman, William. *How to Get the Right Job in Publishing.* Chicago: Contemporary Books, 1983.
A field-specific publication with an excellent overview and advice on job hunting for positions in newspapers, magazines, book publishing, etc.

Schmidt, Peggy, Editor. *Career Choices for Students of* New York: Walker & Company, 1985.
A series of books addressing career options by majors, including art, business communications and journalism, computer science, economics, history, mathematics, political science and government, and psychology. Each book presents about six to eight career field options and describes entry-level opportunities, qualifications, job responsibilities, salary information, recommended readings, and professional associations related to each field. Brief interviews with persons in the respective fields are also included.

Stumpf, Stephen, and Celeste K. Rodgers. *Choosing a Career in Business.* New York: Fireside Books, 1984.
Covers commercial banking, securities analysis, investment banking, corporate finance, accounting, product management, advertising, communications and public relations, sales, human resource management, systems analysis, and business consulting. Each field is covered in a separate chapter that provides enough information to give focus to those who "want to do something in business" but do not yet know what. A collection of bibliographies related to each chapter appears at the end of the book, as does a list of basic job resources.

Wright, John W. *The American Almanac of Jobs and Salaries.* New York: Avon Books, 1984.
A collection of information on job descriptions and salary ranges for numerous fields. Used creatively, the book can help you become aware of career paths and the financial rewards of moving up job ladders.

Appendix

This appendix consists of reproducible copies of the flowcharts and exercises used in the resume-writing and interview processes. Readers are encouraged to make use of these tools in their own job search efforts.

Chronological Flowchart

DATES	EDUCATIONAL HISTORY	NOTABLE ACHIEVEMENTS AND ACTIVITIES	EMPLOYMENT HISTORY

Skills Inventory

1. Analytical Realm

ANALYZING AND EVALUATING
___quantitative or statistical data
___services or programs
___performances of groups or individuals
___value of objects or services

CLASSIFYING
___objects or people into categories
___status of applicants or applications

ESTIMATING AND APPRAISING
___cost of services or programs
___time requirements of services to be performed or programs to take place
___physical space required of services or programs

___number of persons or items required for services or programs

EXAMINING
___financial records
___procedures and policies
___physical objects or locations

RESEARCHING
___information from libraries or written sources
___information from obscure sources
___backgrounds of groups or individuals
___historical information
___information from people via interviews
___information from physical evidence
___information for immediate uses
___information for continued research

2. Communications Realm

BUYING
___for resale to the public
___for resale to distributors or retailers
___for use by organizations or for events

CORRESPONDING
___by answering inquiries by mail or phone
___by initiating contact by mail or phone

DISTRIBUTING
___to persons one-on-one
___to places for resale

EDITING
___book manuscripts
___newspaper or magazine articles

___papers, reports, or proposals
___for grammatical errors
___for style or format

INTERPRETING AND TRANSLATING
___languages
___technical data into lay terms
___complicated ideas into clear language

READING AND PROOFREADING
___large amounts of information quickly
___for errors or style
___to synthesize abstracts

REPRESENTING AND RECRUITING
___representing an organization to the public
___recruiting employees or volunteers
___promoting a point of view, soliciting funds or aid

SELLING
___products or ideas one-on-one
___products or ideas to large groups
___in a store
___door-to-door
___by phone
___products or services in high demand
___products or services where demand is created

SPEAKING
___publicly to audiences
___in small groups
___by developing or using presentation materials

WRITING
___copy for sales or advertising
___fiction
___essays
___reports or proposals
___journalistic copy for print or broadcast
___abstracts synthesized from volumes of data or other information
___quickly under deadline pressure
___slowly for accuracy, style, and content

3. Creative Realm

ARRANGING AND DISPLAYING
___materials and equipment for a show
___furniture and fixtures
___products for sale
___wall or window displays
___landscapes

DESIGNING
___layouts for newspapers or magazines
___layouts for advertising or promotional artwork
___brochures, flyers, or posters
___artwork
___audiovisual materials

PERFORMING
___in a theatrical production
___in a musical production
___in a promotional demonstration

PRINTING
___using standard equipment and processes
___using desktop software and hardware
___freehand or in calligraphy

SKETCHING, PAINTING, AND PHOTOGRAPHING
___diagrams, charts, or graphs
___pictures of people or things
___illustrations for a story, idea, proposal, or report
___for artistic purposes
___for advertising or promotional purposes

4. Interactive Realm

COACHING, DIRECTING, AND TUTORING
___athletic teams
___theatrical productions
___academic subjects

COUNSELING AND ADVISING
___on personal problems
___on academic issues
___on financial issues
___as resource person, referring to professionals or to reference materials
___groups or clubs within an academic environment

HANDLING COMPLAINTS
___by listening and responding verbally
___by listening and responding in writing
___by reading and corresponding
___by taking actions
___by calming tense situations

INTERVIEWING
___to determine attitudes

___to gather employment information
___to collect sales or marketing data

MEETING THE PUBLIC
___by receiving and greeting
___by giving tours
___by displaying or selling products
___by conducting surveys in person
___by conducting telephone surveys

TEACHING AND TRAINING
___in a classroom or academic setting
___in a recreational setting
___in a business setting
___groups
___individuals
___physical activities and sports
___academic subjects
___self-improvement
___work-related performance skills and ideas

5. Organizational Realm

MANAGING
___the performance and productivity of others
___information or data collection
___activities of groups or individuals
___by delegating tasks
___a store
___an event

PLANNING
___an event
___a trip

___a system or program
___sales, advertising, or promotional activities
___based on cost/benefit or financial criteria

RECORDKEEPING
___numerical data
___files and records
___database systems

SUPERVISING AND OVERSEEING
___work of others

___physical plants,
apartments, or
buildings
___systems and procedures
___policies and programs

TIMING
___tasks to be completed
in a given period
___events to begin and end
as planned
___efficiency of others

UPDATING
___information for day-
to-day use
___filing systems
___policies and
procedures
___biographical
information
___databases

6. Physical Realm

ATHLETICS
___performing or coaching
a sport or event
___demonstrating or
selling equipment
___planning or promoting
an event
___managing business
aspects

CONSTRUCTING
___houses or buildings
___mechanical or electronic
devices

___objects, such as
furniture, fences, or
platforms

PROTECTING
___people
___objects or buildings

REPAIRING
___mechanical or
electrical devices
___cars or trucks
___home or building
components

7. Quantitative Realm

ACCOUNTING AND
BOOKKEEPING
___maintaining financial
balances
___maintaining accounts
receivable and payable
___tracking sales revenues
versus costs
___keeping records of
actions or transactions
versus costs

BUDGETING
___costs of projects or
systems
___monitoring spending
___developing cost-saving
techniques or plans

CALCULATING
___by hand or with a
simple calculator

COMPUTING AND
DATA PROCESSING
___using desktop
computers
___using laptop
computers
___using mainframes
___for simple
calculations
___for statistical
analyses
___for database
management

_____using packaged
software
_____writing software and
programming
_____explaining hardware or
software to others

8. Scientific Realm

LABORATORY AND
MEDICAL WORK
_____setting up equipment
or instruments
_____using equipment or
instruments
_____designing controlled
experiments
_____caring for laboratory
animals
_____handling specimens
_____inspecting objects or
specimens

_____examining people or
animals

MEASURING
_____to obtain accurate
readings from devices
_____to assess skills or
conditions

TREATING AND
DIAGNOSING
_____animals
_____humans

Summary of Skills Inventory Findings

List fifteen actions that are most job related—those you would most like to utilize in the performance of your job.

_____

_____

_____

_____

_____

_____

_____

_____

_____

_____

_____

_____

_____

_____

_____

List the nine Major Skills that you judge most job related.

_____

_____

_____

_____

_____

_____

_____

_____

_____

Skills Flowchart

EXPERIENCE	BASIC SKILLS AND ACTIONS	SKILLS HEADINGS
		Note: Create Skills Headings by grouping the information listed under Basic Skills and Actions into several broad working categories. You can use Major Skills Categories appearing in the Skills Inventory as well as others. Once completed, these can appear as general headings for functional resumes or functional components of combination resumes.

Job Target Chart

FIELD/JOB TITLE	FUNCTIONAL DESCRIPTION	RELEVANT EXPERIENCES, SKILLS, AND INTERVIEW LINKAGES

Pre-Interview Resume Exercise

Before each interview reproduce the following exercise on the back of your resume in order to organize your thoughts and determine what to highlight during the interview, thus focusing your liberal arts power. Have it available to review prior to your interview. The more you know about yourself, the job, and the potential employer, the more powerful you will be. As a liberal arts job seeker, as an educated communicator, you have the responsibility and the response-ability to do well in each interview you have.

First: Note the following divisions and headings on the back of your resume.

Company:	
Job:	Me:
Functions and Responsibilities:	Skills and Experiences:
1)	1)
2)	2)
3)	3)
4)	4)
5)	5)
6)	6)
3 Major Points:	
3 Anecdotes or Examples:	

Second: Identify the company and position, and detail the job responsibilities and functions. Three to six basic functions and responsibilities should suffice, but feel free to include as many as you judge necessary. For this as well as the other sections use shorthand to make the data fit, but be as detailed as possible.

Third: Identify skills you possess that match the functions and responsibilities. Note your skills as well as the experiences where you developed and used them. Also, cite examples of when skills were used to accomplish particular tasks. When completing this portion for the first time, refer frequently to the front of your resume to recall appropriate skills and experiences. Then, refer to your Skills Inventory, Skills Flowchart, and Job Target Chart to fill in any missing elements.

Fourth: Identify three major points you want to make in the interview. These can be a summary of related skills, references to specific experiences, analyses of particular industry trends or issues, or whatever points you believe are critical. A major point is one you *must* make (perhaps more than once) if you are to judge the interview as a success. Once identified, be sure that you do indeed make these points!

Fifth: Identify three anecdotes or examples that illustrate your qualifications for the job. These can be stories that tell of your uncovering specific issues while conducting research for the interview, reviews of past experiences, sincere expressions of motivations, or interesting examples of your most significant accomplishments. You are not trying to "preprogram" yourself for the interview, but you *are* preparing yourself to recall examples, verbal proof that you have the skills and qualities to do the job successfully. Throughout the interview, you should be painting a verbal picture of yourself as someone capable of performing the functions and responsibilities cited. The more the interviewer perceives you as possessing these capabilities, the greater your chances of obtaining an offer.

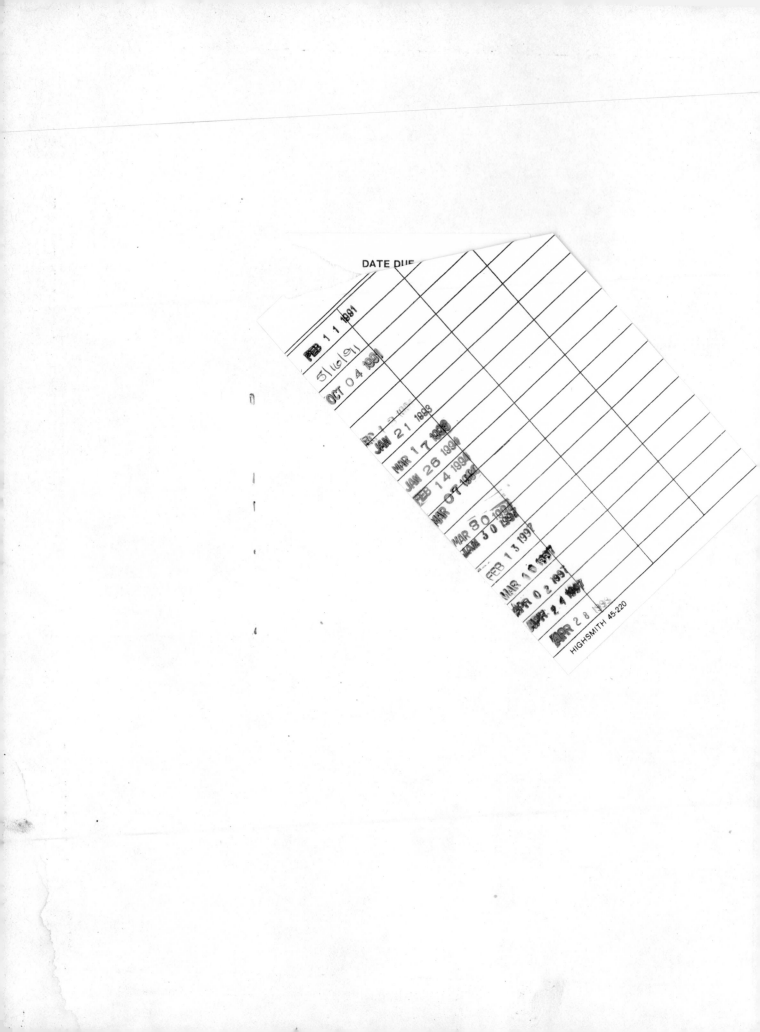

DATE DUE

FEB 11 1991
5|46|91|
OCT 04 1991

JAN 21 1993
MAR 17 1996
MAR 26 1996
JAN 14 1997
FEB OT 1996
MAR 30 1996
MAR 30 1997
FEB 13 1997
MAR 10 1997
MAR 02 1997
APR 24 1997
APR 28 1997

HIGHSMITH 45-220